Anointed WHORE

I pray that this book will help you discover all that God has placed within you.

Be blessed
Jiri

A BOOK OF DELIVERANCE

DR. LISA D. WILLIAMS

~ *L*IVE PUBLISHING ~

Anointed WHORE

A BOOK OF DELIVERANCE

Scripture quotations, unless otherwise noted, are taken from *The King James Version* of the Holy Bible, © 1990 by Thomas Nelson, Inc. Scripture quotations marked (TLB) are taken from *The Living Bible,* © 1971 owned by assignment by KNT Charitable Trust. Scripture quotations marked (NKJV) are taken from *The New King James Version,* © 1979, 1980, 1982, 1991 by Thomas Nelson, Inc. Word definitions are taken from Webster's Ninth New Collegiate Dictionary, © 1991 by Merriam-Webster, Inc.

*L*ive Publishing, LLC
P.O.Box 1622
Jackson, MS 39215

Cover Design *by Damion R. Portis*
Author Photographs *by Will Sterling Photography*

ISBN–13: 978–0–9799112–0–0
ISBN–10: 0–9799112–0–6
LCCN: 2008901701

*In grateful thoughts of my beloved
father, Mr. Sylvester Williams.*

*In funny thoughts of my beloved
sister, Debra R. Terry.*

I miss you both.

TABLE OF CONTENTS

As a well-known singer and choir director at a magnificent place of worship, I have the privilege of leading God's people into the realm of worship and praise. When God began to share with me the message of *Anointed Whore*, I asked Him why He chose me to deliver such a powerful and exposing message. He reminded me that, indeed, I had experienced that walk of life. There were times when I sang under the powerful and transforming anointing, and people would be led into His very presence; but I would immediately leave church and begin walking contrary to His Word.

As time passed, I began to recall some alarming experiences that made me want to repent all over again. I realized how I could be used to draw people to Jesus Christ but was at risk of losing my own soul. God showed me a vision of a Judgment Day scenario of someone being told, "Depart, ye worker of iniquity." That got my attention.

The Holy Spirit revealed to me that I was not acting alone. I realized that there were many others who were anointed and proclaiming the Gospel through singing, preaching, counseling, evangelizing, and other ministries; who were operating by those same standards. As time passed, I knew I had to answer the call to bring this topic to the forefront and remind God's people that He is requiring of us a full-time walk of holiness—a walk that continues even when the public ministry is over. According to Hosea 4:12 and 5:4, *"the spirit of whoredoms hath caused them to err, and they have gone a whoring from under their God...They will not frame their doings to turn unto their God: for the spirit of whoredoms is in the midst of them, and they have not known the Lord."* We are anointed, that is, endowed with the Holy Spirit to fulfill God's calling. However, like the children of Israel, we periodically find ourselves turning away from God and falling into the spirit of whoredom, which is opposing God's will. When an anointed vessel assumes a spirit of whoredom, a worker of iniquity is manifested.

Now, the tricky thing about this is that in some cases, many saints are not even aware that they are balancing their walk between two realms: the realms of worldliness and of holiness. They have become so immune to the conviction of the Holy Spirit that they are ministering through their sin. Others may know they are operating in both worlds but do not know how to get out! They are praying for someone to understand, explain what is happening, and even provide some deliverance tools.

This is why this book pulls the cover back and reveals the tactics of the enemy. We must understand that Satan has studied us and knows what causes us to fall. Therefore, instead of attempting to pull us away from the church, he uses the church as another vehicle to keep us bound.

The devil is neither afraid nor concerned with our anointing; especially if he knows we are committed to him when the service is over. Satan is having a field day at church, and if he can get us wrapped up in church work and Sunday morning "performances" causing us to forget about our souls, then he wins.

You see, the devil does not have to look beyond the sacred walls of the church to find a woman who is willing to have an affair with her married pastor—he uses one who is sitting in the pews. He does not have to hunt for people who will focus on deception and deceit—he knows he can use some committee and ministry leaders to do that.

He knows how easy it is for us to get preoccupied with programs, conferences, appreciations, and anniversaries with little emphasis on pointing people to Jesus Christ. Instead, they become avenues for planting spirits of jealousy, envy, strife, self-promotion, competition, and all other spirits of whoredom—right in the church and in the name of Jesus Christ. When this happens, the Spirit of the Lord departs.

1 Samuel, 15:26, records: *"And Samuel said unto Saul, I will not return with thee: for thou hast rejected the word of the Lord, and the Lord hath rejected thee from being king over Israel."* *"But the Spirit of the Lord had left Saul, and instead, the Lord had sent a tormenting spirit that filled him with desperation and fear"* (1 Sam. 16:14, TLB). When Saul was anointed king of Israel, the Spirit of God was with him as he operated in the will of God.

When he became disobedient, and pride and jealousy became his driving force, God removed His Spirit. Unfortunately, Saul was expected to continue his duties as king although he no longer had an anointing to do so. This is where many of us are now. We are working in ministries and worshipping in places where God's Spirit has already departed. This is one of the setups that lead us into spiritual harlotry.

This book is written with church people in mind. Yes, it is for those who are already working in the church and understand the importance of salvation but may not have a right relationship with God. It is designed to (1) show how one is lured into a lifestyle of spiritual harlotry, (2) provide biblical principles that support a process of deliverance, and (3) offer spiritual insight and encouragement for walking continuously in holiness.

I am determined to remind God's people that those who walk in the anointing of the Lord must also be willing to abide in His way. There is no one who can stop you from walking in both realms. The decision is yours. Just know that any true anointing destroys the yoke, and the same anointing that is used to minister to others is available for your deliverance. God has the power to make us all free. Let's walk through this together.

PART I

HOW IT ALL BEGINS

WHAT HAPPENS WHEN YOU ARE THE PREACHER OR THE PRAISE LEADER, AND YOU ARE ALSO A THIEF OR AN ADULTERER? WHAT HAPPENS WHEN YOU TALK TO YOUR FRIENDS ABOUT HOLINESS, BUT YOU ARE UNCLEAN?

IN ORDER TO EFFECTIVELY WIN SOULS FOR THE KINGDOM, WE MUST UNCOVER THE HIDDEN SINS THAT KEEP US BOUND. THIS SOUL WRENCHING PROCESS IS PAINFUL AND REQUIRES TOTAL SUBMISSION TO GOD.

THIS SECTION COMPELS YOU TO WALK THROUGH YOUR LIFE'S JOURNEY TO IDENTIFY AND UNCOVER THOSE DISTRACTIONS THAT HAVE PREVENTED YOU FROM MOVING INTO A MORE HONEST RELATIONSHIP WITH GOD. THIS IS THE BEGINNING OF DELIVERANCE.

ONE

HAPPY FAULTS

"Who can understand his errors? cleanse thou me from secret faults. Keep back thy servant also from presumptuous sins; let them not have dominion over me: then shall I be upright, and I shall be innocent from the great transgression" (Ps. 19:12–13).

They show up when your spiritual highs begin to simmer. They come when you are weak and need to rest. They sneak up in the middle of work, church, or even during a brief phone conversation. They are good *to* you but not good *for* you. And since they provide a thrilling sense of false fulfillment, the very elect will surrender to them. They are those hidden actions, raging addictions, and embedded desires that satisfy your flesh while causing you to ignore your love for God. One of my dear friends calls them *happy faults*, which are self-destructive relationships in my case.

One summer, I committed myself to a long period of spiritual consecration. I literally spent most of my time in prayer, fasting and studying God's Word. Every morning, I anointed myself, laid on my prayer blanket, and began a three to five hour period of meditation. I could literally see myself growing in the Lord.

I would walk into a place, and people would say things like "His glory is upon you" or "I can tell you have been praying." And when someone senses the fellowship between you and God, then you must be on your way! At least you think you are. However, immediately after this period of consecration, I found myself having to call someone to get rescued from an old, self-destructive relationship!

Now, isn't it strange that after weeks, even months of consecration, it only took the right temptation to mess me up? This one happy fault separated me from God. I emphasize the separation because sometimes we forget that sin separates us from God. It does not matter how close we are to Him or how long we have sacrificed our time or money, sin separates us.

This separation was temporary and was not powerful enough to make me backslide, but because of who I am in God, it tore me down. It took days for me to feel comfortable enough to even approach God. In fact, I was the choir director at my church and was expected to conduct a weekly rehearsal, and at the same time, I was struggling with this fault.

One night, during this same period of regret, a choir rehearsal was quickly approaching. I went into the church, said a quick prayer at the altar and began to teach the songs of praise. Not only did I teach the music, but I also encouraged the members to continue this walk of faith when, certainly, my gift was the only thing that qualified me to stand in front of them. There was no true preparation and no connection with God. In essence, I was just doing a job. Basically, as happy faults become more routine, your services at church and your walk with God will become more routine. This is where the risks begin.

Let us use King David as an example. When he committed adultery with Bathsheba, he could have repented immediately and turned away, but failing to do so caused Uriah (Bathsheba's husband) to lose his life. David let his happy fault take over his spiritual connection, and he remained in an unrepented state. Remaining there is the trick. The longer the enemy can keep you from repenting, either by guilt or your desire, the more vulnerable you become. The point is this: the time between the sin and true repentance is crucial. You must rush back into the Word and be restored through prayer and faith. If you remain there as David did, you will begin a dangerous walk of ministering through thorns. And like David, you will probably add another charge to the list.

TWO

MINISTERING THROUGH THORNS

*"They shall be as thorns in your sides, and their gods
shall be a snare unto you" (Judg. 2:3).*

Even though I knew God would forgive me for yielding to
my happy fault, that knowledge did not ease the guilt. In fact, it got
worse because I felt unworthy to pray. Little by little, I whispered
to God like an ashamed little child, "I'm sorry; please don't be
mad too long, forgive me." Although I knew He would, it just felt
like He was tired of me; therefore, it took me longer to get back on
track. This was perilous!

When you have to stand and minister before others while
you are caught up yourself, you are at a make or break point, and
you must not stay there! It is urgent that you start praying and telling yourself to get back to God. This season is deadly because

when a person ministers through thorns, the production of the ministry looks the same—the people will continue to get saved, the altars will still be flooded with sinners, your Sunday school students will still show up, the thunders of praise will still roar through the church, the tithes and offerings will still be brought, you will still drive your Mercedes, your reputation and witness will still be respected. And even though this is "all good," you can be fooled and find yourself depressed, oppressed, and overpowered by the enemy. In other words, you are in sinking sand and do not even know it!

When you minister through thorns, you are in a dangerous situation. Because you are in a state of regression, you run the risks of missing your purpose, hindering others from seeing God, and losing your sensitivity to discern.

MISSING YOUR PURPOSE

Everything we receive from God must be received through faith and in the spiritual realm. The scripture is clear when it states that God is a Spirit. This means that everything about Him and from Him will be released in the spiritual realm. And if we are to receive and ever fulfill our purpose, then we must be in a position where God can communicate with us. God has designed for us a specific purpose or reason for ministry, but if we walk in carnality, we will certainly miss it.

"Because the carnal mind is enmity against God: for it is not subject to the law of God, neither indeed can be. So then they that are in the flesh cannot please God" (Rom. 8:7–8). God has a master plan, but He does not release it to our flesh. He knows that our flesh is incapable of interpreting it and will aggressively deny it. Your flesh and God's purpose will never live as one. This is why you must sacrifice any iniquity that separates you from God's will. If you regress and begin to operate in the sins of your past, then you will miss your purpose.

Have you ever listened to a familiar preacher whose sermons were suddenly moving in a weird direction? I mean, all of a sudden, he or she was calling right wrong and wrong right! Perhaps, even his or her actions and decisions were *worldly* and totally out of spiritual character. If so, you were probably witnessing a preacher who, because of flesh, was ministering against an ordained purpose.

When this happens, one or more things will occur: the minister will not grow spiritually, will begin to implement his or her own purpose, or will become completely ineffective, that is, lose the platform.

Let us take a look at one of God's major servants, Moses. Now, I write this portion with care because I know that everyone loves Moses and his courageous leadership style. I am aware that he is the prophet who stood before Pharaoh, crossed the Red Sea, and even asked God to show him His glory. Yet, he is the same prophet who forfeited a walk in the Promised Land because he responded to his flesh. This part of Moses' ministry should not be ignored, tragic but relevant:

And Moses and Aaron went from the presence of the assembly unto the door of the tabernacle of the congregation, and they fell upon their faces: and the glory of the Lord appeared unto them.

And the Lord spake unto Moses, saying,

Take the rod, and gather thou the assembly together, thou, and Aaron thy brother, and speak ye unto the rock before their eyes; and it shall give forth his water, and thou shalt bring forth to them water out of the rock: so thou shalt give the congregation and their beasts drink.

And Moses took the rod from before the Lord, as he commanded him.

And Moses and Aaron gathered the congregation together before the rock, and he said unto them, Hear now, ye rebels; must we fetch you water out of this rock?

And Moses lifted up his hand, and with his rod he smote the rock twice: and the water came out abundantly, and the congregation drank, and their beasts also.

And the Lord spake unto Moses and Aaron, Because ye

believed me not, to sanctify me in the eyes of the children of Israel, therefore ye shall not bring this congregation into the land which I have given them. (Num. 20:6–12)

Can you see what happened here? Moses indeed positioned himself spiritually to hear from the Lord, and God released the answer. But this is what really happened—Moses only dealt with the need for water and the rebelliousness of the people as opposed to God's need to be sanctified. He therefore responded to his own flesh and proceeded to strike the rock instead of speaking to it. Moses could not perceive that God was doing a new thing, pushing him to another level. This is what happens when you regress in the middle of your ministry: you will miss the fullness of your purpose! You must be ready to move with the flow of God and do what is expected.

Now consider this. When Moses struck the rock, the water was abundantly released to the people and their flock. (As mentioned earlier, the production would continue to look good.) But this one bad decision led to the death of Aaron and sent the entire nation of Israel into a period of mourning. Had Moses obeyed the command, he would have experienced a new level of ministry and would have fulfilled the purpose of sanctifying God before the people.

HINDERING THEM FROM SEEING GOD

So, why was Aaron punished? Aaron did not strike the rock. Moses did. Why was he humiliated and stripped before his sons and the rest of the church? Why did the children of Israel have to experience extended mourning? Numbers 20:23–29 reads:

> *And the Lord spake unto Moses and Aaron in mount Hor, by the coast of the land of E'-dom, saying,*
>
> *Aaron shall be gathered unto his people: for he shall not enter into the land which I have given unto the children of Israel, because ye rebelled against my word at the water of Mer'-i-bah.*
>
> *Take Aaron and E-le-a'-zar his son, and bring them up unto mount Hor:*
>
> *And strip Aaron of his garments, and put them upon E-le-a'-zar his son: and Aaron shall be gathered unto his people, and shall die there.*
>
> *And Moses did as the Lord commanded: and they went up into mount Hor in the sight of all the congregation.*
>
> *And Moses stripped Aaron of his garments, and put them upon E-le-a'-zar his son; and Aaron died there in the top of the mount: and Moses and E-le-a'-zar came down from the mount.*
>
> *And when all the congregation saw that Aaron was*

dead, they mourned for Aaron thirty days, even all the house of Israel.

Those who are anointed to do the work of God must also be accountable. In this case, Moses was not only accountable for his own spiritual development, but he was also accountable for those who followed him. Yes, Aaron was the high priest called of God, but he was still responsible to Moses. Moses was the influence.

Therefore, when you make decisions based on your flesh, as did Moses, you will hinder those around you. As an anointed person of God, like it or not, you become a role model. Your words and actions really do matter. Sinners and saints should be able to look at the men and women of God and see a reflection of Him. We are the only representatives that God has. He is expecting us to walk in holiness, obedience, and integrity!

LOSING THE SENSITIVITY TO DISCERN

As leaders, we must always be sensitive to the Spirit of God. There will be times when God wants to do a complete shifting, and we must be in a place to hear it. Moses was at the edge of that place, but he missed it. God wanted to use the power of *speaking* a command, an unfamiliar and unusual pattern, to produce the resource. In other words, He was changing His way of doing things.

You must understand that this was not the first time Moses

had experienced water being released from a rock: *"Behold, I will stand before thee upon the rock in Ho'-reb; and thou shalt smite the rock, and there shall come water out of it, that the people may drink. And Moses did so in the sight of the elders of Israel"* (Exod.17:6). So, we see that Moses was not surprised when he was instructed at the desert of Zin to use the rock for water. However, because he was acting in his flesh, he was not sensitive to the new move of God. He knew that at the least he could strike the rock and cause it to produce water. And that is what he relied on—his past experience and his flesh—to produce the resource.

Like Moses, many of us as leaders are at that same juncture. This is the place where we risk losing it all. The ministry lies dormant because we are still trying to feed the sheep from an old, familiar source. We do not sense the shifting; therefore, we continue to strike the rock. After all, we know how to do that and are totally comfortable there.

For instance, there are many leaders who have been instructed to redirect the focus and pattern of service and even seek other avenues for their resources, but they are stuck in old ways and refuse to do it. They have not accepted the fact that God is sovereign and must not be limited. Therefore, they remain in a place of comfort, and they strike the rock!

Nevertheless, there will be times in your life when God will do a shifting. Perhaps, it will be with your finances, your relationships, or your ministry. The key is to be able to discern what He is doing. In order to do so, you must remain in communion with God, not only listening to Him, but also acting on His Word. Remember, God wants to be glorified in your life. He wants you to *speak* to the rock. As stated earlier, ministering through thorns is risky religious business. It is what the devil wants you to become comfortable with; but for the sake of your soul and the souls of others, you cannot afford to get comfortable.

For the deliverance process to begin, you must first fully acknowledge your transgressions and know that your sin is ever before God. When I took this step in my life, God not only began to restore me, but He renewed my spirit and revived my soul— *"where sin abounded, grace did much more abound"* (Rom. 5:20). What a merciful Father.

THREE

THERE IS A ROOT—CHURCH FIGHTS!

"And now also the ax is laid unto the root of the trees: therefore every tree which bringeth not forth good fruit is hewn down, and cast into the fire" (Matt. 3:10).

Every tree has a root, and every turn—right or wrong—has a beginning. As I think about the beginning, I am reminded of my younger years as a member of a Mississippi Baptist Church. This church established my perception of God and my understanding of religion. It was complete with great preaching, good teaching, awesome singing, and do not forget the shouting! We had an excellent children's department, Sunday school department, and everything else that comes with a church. And although it seemed like the perfect place, there was another side. There were times when holy hands would be lifted on Sunday mornings, and those same hands were scuffling later on, especially during what was called "church meetings."

I clearly remember the church meetings. They were generally held to discuss the business of the church, yet at times they seemed to turn into church fights, literally! At the beginning of the meetings, someone would read a general report, and everything would appear to be okay. Then, out of the blue, it seemed, the action would begin!

Although, there was one *special* church meeting that stood above them all. As I remember, one night my sisters and I were instructed to get dressed for church. Based on the conversations I overheard, I knew this meeting would be very different. On the way to the church, everyone was quiet but anxious, I recall. Since I was only a young girl, I did not have a clue as to what to expect or how to brace myself during the span of the next hour.

When we arrived at the church and began to walk inside, I could hear someone apprehensively say, "She has a gun in her coat! It's a .38!" At the time, I did not know who said it, nor did I know who had the gun. I only knew that fear gripped my little body as I began to nervously look around. Then one of my sisters snatched me to my seat, and we waited for the meeting to begin.

The first fifteen minutes of the meeting were truly about business. Then, as stated earlier, the atmosphere began to change. I could hear whispers and even noticed that my sisters began to look disturbed. I looked at my mom and could sense the same discomfort. At the same time, I noticed that one of the women in the church was approaching the microphone. She spoke for several minutes and towards the end of her comments, she called out our family name, and this set it off! My family became infuriated, and one of my sisters jumped up and threatened everybody in the church! Then the screaming, pushing, and jerking began—all in the sanctuary. At this point, my knees were shaking so fiercely that they could have been heard above all of the noise! I remember thinking, "This is a good place, and this should not be happening here..." I was so scared and confused.

This was one of the first lessons that taught me that we can preach, sing, work for the Lord and still be outrageous! This was a powerful seed that was planted. And because it was rooted and fostered in the church, it somehow seemed justified. In time, it all blended in and was a part of the normal church life.

In retrospect, I understand that the enemy's plan was to paint a picture that could eventually confuse me, abort what God had predestined for me, and cancel the blessings my mother spoke over my life. You see, my mother prayed for me as she carried me. She declared before I was born that I would receive a double portion of God's best. She asked God to give to me everything that He had for her and for me. Then she named me Lisa, which means "consecrated to God." Oh yes, the groundwork was set. But just as she prayed, Satan also began his plan to steal, kill, and destroy me.

You must understand that when you were born, God's plan for you was already determined, and everything you needed to be prosperous was already placed within you. Jeremiah 1:5 reads, *"Before I formed thee in the belly I knew thee; and before thou camest forth out of the womb I sanctified thee, and I ordained thee a prophet unto the nations."* However, just like God predestined your purpose, the devil's plan for you was also set in motion.

Please know that Satan does not wait until we are mature in age or mature in the Lord to kill us. He tries to destroy us immediately! He wants us when we are babies, sitting in church exposed to the facades of life. Hopefully, you will be covered in prayer and protected by the Master's love. And, as stated earlier, the roots of my religious beliefs were established at a church. Thankfully, it included long-lasting relationships, strong teachings of the Word, and a faith that will remain with me forever. I'm grateful.

CAN'T DESCRIBE THIS FEELING

Between the period of *church fights* and my teenage years, somehow God found a quiet place within my spirit, and He began to stir up what He had placed within me before I was born. I remember one Sunday on my thirteenth birthday, I led a song, and at the end of the song I began to cry. I experienced a warm, overwhelming sense of gratitude to God, and a strong feeling of protection rested upon me. At that moment, I believe God was confirming that He loved me and would always be with me. I cannot say that I felt a call on my life; I simply knew that I had something special living within me.

As I continued singing and crying, my mother stood behind me and began rubbing my back, assuring me that it was okay to express myself in this way. She knew that this was a new experience, and I was possibly afraid. In retrospect, I understand that God was establishing a point of connection with me that was exclusive and life-changing. He was using this experience to show me that there was more to Him than what I had experienced at church.

Here is the key: God began to implant a hunger for His Spirit within me. Each Sunday, I wanted to get that same feeling that I felt as I sang on my thirteenth birthday, but that did not happen. Most of the time, it was church as usual. Naturally, since I received that warm sensation while singing, I tried to connect with that feeling through the songs.

Eventually, this search for that feeling led me into pure entertainment. I took singing to the next level! I started adding hand gestures, jumping up and down, spinning around, and anything else I could. I wanted that feeling, and for a while, the attention of the crowd gave it to me. Although it was a pseudo-high, it was an awesome replacement.

As the years passed, my family eventually joined another church. I was a little more mature, so I felt closer to reaching the fulfillment I was searching for. However, in this place in my life, the little knowledge I had was dangerous. I became like so many others have become—a basic church member. I had zeal, or I desired God, but I did not fully receive Him. I did not know the significance of the Trinity—the Father, Son and Holy Ghost. I did not understand the true power of the resurrection and the requirement of purification. This made me vulnerable, and I began to fall into traps and things that looked like God but were not.

While I knew more about God, He was still like a fairy-tale to me. I was very familiar with the God who delivered Daniel from the den of lions and the three Hebrew boys from the fire, but something was missing. In essence, I was floating around with the standards that were planted within me at the first church, a musical gift, and the teachings learned from the new church, but something was *still* missing.

My ears heard the Word, but my eyes were fixed on the church members. This is how new converts and weak Christians miss the mark. We begin to build relationships with the preachers and members but never develop one with God. When this happens, we actually become separated from God. The desire to be connected with Him may exist, but we never actually make that connection.

These are the perfect conditions for the anointed whore to develop. In this place, we are still in search of something that has not yet manifested. So, as we continue in ministry, we also begin to generate and offer up "strange fire."

FOUR

STRANGE FIRE

"And Na'-dab and A-bi'-hu, the sons of Aaron, took either of
them his censer, and put fire therein, and put incense thereon, and offered
strange fire before the Lord, which He commanded them not. And there
went out fire from the Lord, and devoured them, and they died before the
Lord" (Lev.10:1–2).

When God begins to use you in the building up of His
Kingdom, your flesh will want to see physical evidence of His
power; therefore, you have to be careful not to try to replace it with
something that only resembles it. If we offer our gifts acting on our
own strength and motives, God will reject those offerings because
they are not of Him.

As we see in Leviticus, Nadab and Abihu knew that God
required holy, sacrificial offerings. They knew that the system of

sacrifices was extensive and established by God alone. Yet, they took it upon themselves to use their position as ordained priests to orchestrate a prideful offering. They did not receive the command from God, nor did they sacrifice or lose anything. They did not render burnt offerings, peace offerings, sin offerings, or grain offerings. They simply walked up to God and said, *"Here, God, take this."* How can we worship without sacrifice? How can we worship except it be in spirit and truth?

There can be no worship and fellowship without sacrifice. You can work in ministries, dance, sing, and preach without making a sacrifice, but you cannot worship and fellowship with God without making a sacrifice. There is a clear difference. This is why I am convinced that those who say they are worshippers have also given up some things. Nobody can truly stand before the presence of the Almighty God and remain the same!

You should lose something every time you enter His presence. A lying spirit is lost, a gambling spirit is lost, a worrying spirit is lost, a stingy spirit is lost. Addictions are destroyed, lack is destroyed, anger is destroyed. Something is lost! A sacrifice has to be made. It is then that the Lord communes with us and shows us His glory. Anything that is offered outside of that process is *strange fire*. God knows when the worship and offerings are holy and sacrificial. He knows when the motives are pure.

If your worship and gifts are offered by any other means,

like Nadab and Abihu, you will have used the priestly appointment and the anointing that is upon your life to gratify yourself. God will not accept it. In fact, you may even receive His wrath.

FIVE

PROSTITUTING THE ANOINTING

"Who exchanged the truth of God for the lie, and worshiped and served the creature rather than the Creator, who is blessed forever" (Rom.1:25, NKJV).

When you use godly principles through ungodly motives, you are prostituting the anointing. *Prostitution* in its natural connotation is the act of deliberately making an exchange of one's natural gift for something in return. *To prostitute* also means "to devote to corrupt or unworthy purposes" (Webster). In this case, it means to use a holy thing for the purpose of self-promotion.

This behavior is prevalent in the church, but we do not talk about it. The anointing should be used to glorify God and lead people to Jesus Christ. However, many times we use it in order to appear spiritually connected or powerful in the eyes of men. We will consciously make a clear decision to misuse the power of God.

As a singer, there were times when I would ask God to *forgive me my sins and anoint me* only minutes before singing. In pure honesty, some of the time, I was not asking for the anointing in order to reach the hearts of men. I believe, however, that I wanted the anointing so that I could receive the praise of men. I never wanted to hear anyone say, "Lisa can sing, but she is not anointed." In essence, the anointing was going to be used to momentarily promote me, not change me or them.

If you are honest, you may be able to recall times when you wanted the anointing only to be elevated and approved in the eyes of men. You were not really concerned about their souls and whether they received the heart of the message. You just wanted to look good and sound good in front of them.

We were called out and anointed to become true workers in the Kingdom. Everything we do should point people to Jesus Christ. If we misuse the ability to minister, we are as bad as Simon the sorcerer who, when he saw Peter and John lay hands on the Samaritans, wanted to purchase the same power:

Give me also this power, that on whomsoever I lay hands, he may receive the Holy Ghost.

But Peter said unto him, Thy money perish with thee, because thou hast thought that the gift of God may be purchased with money.

Thou hast neither part nor lot in this matter: for thy heart is not right in the sight of God.

Repent therefore of this thy wickedness, and pray God, if perhaps the thought of thine heart may be forgiven thee. (Acts 8:19–22)

The power of God is not for sale; neither should it be connected to anything that is self-promoting. Simon wanted the rights to *showboat* in the land. He wanted people calling his secretary to schedule appointments for *Holy Ghost sessions*! Think about the money he would have made! Simon was clearly going to pervert the purpose of the Holy Spirit to promote himself.

Do you know anyone like that? Have you seen any apostles, preachers, or teachers that claim the rights to the Holy Ghost? Have you heard any church commercials that offer the gifts of the Holy Spirit in exchange for something? This is pure prostitution in the name of the church.

We do not own God's power. Yes, He has given us knowledge and authority, but we do not have the right to exploit it or re-define it. The Spirit of God cannot be jailed and released at one's own will. Your motive must be lined up with the mission of the church and the purpose of glorifying God.

For those who are misusing the anointing, there is good

news. If you read closely the conversation with Peter and Simon, you will find that Peter told Simon that if he repented and asked God to clean his heart, he would be forgiven. It was just that simple. This is still true today. If you have found yourself in the "spotlight" of ministry, God is still willing to clean your heart and forgive you. You must be willing to expose the motive and allow God to begin His perfect work in you. When this has occurred, pure motives and pure ministry can truly take place.

Dear Father,

It is with a humble spirit and mind that we ask for Your forgiveness and mercy. We admit that at times we have been unfaithful in our assignments, and that we have walked in our flesh. But now, we are making a decision to be renewed in an honest relationship with You.

Fill us with Your Holy Spirit, wash us in the blood of Jesus, and let Your Word rule our heart, mind, body, and soul. We ask for Your wisdom and strength to walk in full integrity and pray for opportunities to prove our faithfulness to You.

In Jesus' name,
Amen.

PART II

THE POWER OF RELIGIOUS INFLUENCES—EXTERNAL

UNTIL WE EXPOSE HOW THE ENEMY USES RELIGION AS A TOOL TO MANIPULATE OR INFLUENCE SAINTS, WE WILL FOREVER GO THROUGH THE CYCLES OF WALKING IN THE SPIRIT ON SUNDAYS AND WALKING IN THE FLESH ON MONDAYS THROUGH SATURDAYS.

THIS SECTION UNCOVERS THE SPIRITUAL TRAPS AND SETUPS THAT ARE OFTEN IGNORED OR DISGUISED IN THE CHURCH THROUGH THE LEADERS, THROUGH GIFTS AND TALENTS, AND THROUGH MINISTRIES.

IDENTIFYING AND UNDERSTANDING YOUR ROLE IN THE CHURCH ALONGSIDE YOUR ROLE IN PERSONAL DEVELOPMENT IS ESSENTIAL IN TAKING STEPS TO A HIGHER PLACE IN GOD.

SIX

IS THIS THE RIGHT CHURCH?

To the church in Pergamos: *"But I have a few things
against thee, because thou hast there them that
hold the doctrine of Ba'-laam, who
taught Ba'-lac to cast a stumbling block
before the children of Israel, to eat
things sacrificed unto idols, and
to commit fornication" (Rev. 2:14).*

One of the most overlooked elements in our Christian walk
is the evaluation of our church and pastor. Just as you make sure
that your personal motives are pure, you must also be connected to
a church that has pure motives and is equipped to get you ready for
your destiny. This is extremely important because church is the
ideal place for the enemy to lure and lock you into a lifestyle of

anointed whoredom. Your pastor and church must be selected by God. I cannot stress this point enough. Trust me on this: *your pastor and your church must be selected by God.* You cannot select a church or remain at a church based on how good the pastor looks, how well he or she dresses, how good the choir sounds, or how big the building is. This is a spiritual life choice that must be made by God.

As mentioned earlier, church is where one can experience both the carnal and spiritual worlds. It is where I was exposed to sex, alcohol, cigarettes, and all other sorts of sin. I constantly had to battle with whether I could even be spiritual at church! The propositions for committing the same sins were endless. What was interesting is that this behavior never seemed to be perverted or wrong. Most of it was the norm and somewhat accepted.

This is not how God intended for His house to be. Jesus said that it should be a house of prayer, fit for God's name and His presence. You should be able to worship there and hear what the Spirit is saying to the church. It should not be a spiritual whorehouse!

Your place of worship is your corporate tie into the Kingdom. If it operates out of God's will, and you are not strong enough to be an agent for change, you will more than likely take on the spirit of that church. This is why Paul had to warn the Corinthians of allowing sin to operate in the church. He knew that sin was contagious, and that it was even more deadly in the name of the church.

In the fifth chapter of 1 Corinthians, Paul expressed his concern about the outbreak of sin among the saints. He specifically wrote of a man in the church who was having a sexual affair with his own father's wife. Not only was this sin gruesome, but, as Paul said, it was even more horrible because nobody was outraged about it! It was totally acceptable, and the Corinthians were too proud to even address it. In other words, they decided to cover up the sin so that they could look holy before others and continue on with church as usual. However, Paul said, *"Your glorying is not good. Know ye not that a little leaven leaveneth the whole lump? Purge out therefore the old leaven, that ye may be a new lump, as ye are unleavened. For even Christ our passover is sacrificed for us"* (1 Cor. 5:6–7).

The leaven in this scripture symbolizes an evil presence or something that is infected. Not only is Paul condemning the leaven in the church, but he is also reminding us that the smallest portion of leaven can infect the entire body.

In essence, if you are a part of a church that allows, celebrates, or ignores blatant sin, you, too, can be infected. You will begin to blend in with this behavior and before you know it, you will have become a church sinner having no respect for the sacrifice that was made for you.

You must realize that the leaven that Paul spoke of is actually a reminder that spirits are transferable. This spirit of perversion that was allowed to operate among the Corinthians was on its way to infecting the entire church. In fact, fornication in that church was already a common act. Before long, everyone in the church would have been committing fornication, adultery, or any other illegal sexual relationship. Only the spiritually strong would have been able to stand against it.

I know as you are reading now, you can think of a few churches that have been *labeled.* You may know of a church that is known for homosexuality. All of the homosexuals in the city attend this particular church, and every department in that church is run by practicing homosexuals. When this is evident, that church has assumed a spirit of perversion that is totally *at home.* Everyone is comfortable with it, and that spirit is the underlying authority in that church.

1 Corinthians 5:11 records, *"But now I have written unto you not to keep company, if any man that is called a brother be a fornicator, or covetous, or an idolater, or a railer, or a drunkard, or an extortioner; with such an one no not to eat."* The interesting thought in this passage is that Paul was not admonishing us to totally stay away from sinners. That's impossible because we live in the world with everyone. He was clearly speaking of those brothers and sisters who have openly confessed Jesus Christ as Lord. He

was talking about church people.

Remember, the church in the hands of the enemy can be used as a mask or religious meeting place that simply covers sin. You must therefore make sure that you are not walking blindly in a place that has not been selected for you by God.

THE MEETING PLACE

In most cases, the members of a church can be categorized into three sections: (1) Christians who fully understand their purpose and are serious about living the Word, (2) Christians who are attempting to understand their purpose and know how to apply the Word in their lives, and (3) Christians who are just proud to make it in on Sundays.

More than half of the Christians in one or more of those categories are facing integrity and character issues that may not have been tried through God's purification fire. Consequently, when these same people begin to take on positions and join ministries in the church, their true characters are often hidden behind church work; therefore, it looks churchy. However, no purification has taken place. Purification is that process by which God reveals to you your wickedness, cleanses you from your iniquities, and uses the Word to reshape your thoughts and actions by the inner workings of the Holy Spirit.

A person can actually submit to religious work without

having submitted himself to the Lord for inner cleansing. This is why so many people backslide and never see a greater level of living. They join church, go through the right hand of fellowship, have the new member's dinner but do not address the works of the flesh (see Gal. 5). Instead, they have made the church a club, a den of thieves, and just a meeting place. Those who practice such sins might inherit church membership but not the Kingdom.

One of our mistakes is that we miss the course *Crucifixion of Flesh 101.* Instead of working hard to sacrifice our desires, we will abuse the scriptures that describe God as a forgiving God. We say things like "I slipped, but He knows my heart. I'm still going through; I'm not where I ought to be, but I'm not where I used to be." These very words, when used as excuses, can keep us on an elementary level and can eventually assist us straight to hell. I wonder if God will "know your heart" while you are on fire!

Here is the thought. The trap of the *meeting place* is that since we are definitely concerned with our reputation and careful not to hang out with known sinners, we spend our time with the people we see on Sundays—church folks. In many cases, this can be a problem.

Here is what happened to me. When I got saved, became active in the church and made new *holy* friends, my old demons connected with their old demons, and before I knew it, we were all caught up! Church became my meeting place.

I found a church partner who smoked, and we smoked together. I found one who didn't mind cussing, and we cussed together. I found one who wanted to party at the clubs, and we did that also. Sometimes, we would go to church and immediately go straight to the clubs. There we were, a table full of anointed women and men of God, moving and grooving to the devil's beat. You see, we were doing the same things but with different people—church people.

Again, this happened because purification was not the focus when we joined church. Many times, we were more interested in signing up for ministries and learning the rules and regulations of the church instead of working to pull down strongholds. Jesus said:

No man putteth a piece of new cloth unto an old garment, for that which is put in to fill it up taketh from the garment, and the rent is made worse.

Neither do men put new wine into old bottles: else the bottles break, and the wine runneth out, and the bottles perish: but they put new wine into new bottles, and both are preserved. (Matt. 9:16–17)

Everything must be new! If not, even as a church member, you can lose. In other words, you *and* your choir member friends can perish!

Many of the churches today resemble churches described in the second chapter of Revelation. Most of those churches had characteristics of the good and bad. They were faithful in work, service, faith, and love but also participated in idolatry and sexual immorality. The reality of it all is that Jesus is not returning for mixed up churches. He is returning for a church *"not having spot, or wrinkle, or any such thing; but that it should be holy and without blemish"* (Eph. 5:27).

To be spotted is to be stained or tainted "in character or reputation." *To be wrinkled* is to be "imperfect or irregular" (Webster). This means that if we abide in "spotted and wrinkled" places of worship or even allow our personal temples to be damaged by the association, we may miss God.

Here's a look at a few ways that the enemy may use the church to keep you bound and walking in a fake, "religious-looking" journey with God:

- The church participates in good deeds and services, but sexual immorality is practiced and accepted (see Rev. 2:20).

- You are encouraged to participate in religious activities, but you are spiritually dead—there is no push for you to have a relationship with the Father, Son and Holy Spirit (see Rev. 3:1).

- There are strict religious standards in place; yet there is no love for God. All of the attention is placed on methods and doctrines (see Rev. 2:2–4).

- The church has riches, wealth, and "need of nothing" but does not have God (see Rev. 3:17).

By no means is this list conclusive, neither does it tell you to leave your church. It simply offers a close description of a place that may not be moving you forward in the Kingdom. At some point, you have to assess where you are and how you are influenced to grow in God.

Ultimately, the church can either be a place of worship and refuge, or it can be a *meeting place*. Understand that in order to avoid such traps you must be accountable for your spiritual development and for your connection to a church and pastor of truth and sincerity. Both have the power to influence your walk with God.

SEVEN

IS THIS THE RIGHT PASTOR?

"The Lord is my shepherd; I shall not want. He maketh me to lie down in green pastures: he leadeth me beside the still waters. He restoreth my soul: he leadeth me in the paths of righteousness for his name's sake. Yea, though I walk through the valley of the shadow of death, I will fear no evil: for thou art with me; thy rod and thy staff they comfort me. Thou preparest a table before me in the presence of mine enemies: thou anointest my head with oil; my cup runneth over. Surely goodness and mercy shall follow me all the days of my life: and I will dwell in the house of the Lord for ever" (Ps. 23:1–6).

Just as your church is a significant part of your spiritual development, your pastor's role is equally essential. There are many passages of scripture that speak to the duties and responsibilities of those called to be ambassadors and representatives of God. In the

New Testament, Jesus told Peter, *"Feed my lambs...Feed my sheep"* (John 21:15–16). Therefore, the primary role of the pastor is to function as the shepherd of the flock.

The work of the shepherd is manifold, but the primary elements of his or her responsibilities are to feed, water, guide, protect, and restore the sheep. It is a foregone conclusion that in order to function as an effective shepherd, one must have a relationship with Christ through a life of prayer. Jesus said, "I am the good shepherd." Therefore, every pastor's goal or desire should be to emulate Him.

The Lord feeds you through the mouth of your pastor. This is a very powerful position. If you are properly connected, he or she can empower and affirm you. If you are not properly connected, you will become spiritually malnourished or starved. *Malnourished* is defined as provided with "faulty or inadequate nutrition." *To starve* means "to perish from lack of food or to destroy by or cause to suffer from deprivation" (Webster). If you are to live a healthy and complete life in the fullness of God, you must be fed the food of God—His Word.

FEEDING

It is very possible to sit in a church Sunday after Sunday without hearing from God through the preached Word. Because you have become acclimated to the type of message or even the style of delivery from your pastor, you may not be aware that you are not receiving the Word, or that you even need to strongly consider what is being taught. This is why as you are growing spiritually (by studying the Word of God yourself), you must constantly be mindful of your weekly feeding.

Your pastor may know how to *hoop* and excite your emotions, but when the *hoop* is over, ask yourself: what has God said through the Word? Your pastor may even be knowledgeable in a particular area such as business or community development; but if he or she is limited to only that particular message, you may learn how to be an entrepreneur but not how to rebuke sickness or be delivered from drugs through the Word. Do not get me wrong. I love the diversity of sermons and the celebratory (hooping) part; but if the hoop did not teach me the Word, I am going to die! I need something to help me live. Give me the Word!

Ezekiel, chapter 34, highlights God's passion for the duties of shepherds toward the sheep. Ezekiel received an order from God that sent him directly to the shepherds of Israel. God wanted the shepherds to know that He saw them neglecting the souls for whom they were accountable and sending them out to fight the enemy with no assistance, in other words, with no Word or power! Instead of preaching the Word, the pastors were using the pulpit to make money, thrive in the political realm, or manipulate the minds of vulnerable people in order to create their own kingdoms.

In some cases, the pastors even applied the Word to their own lives, yet did not fully teach it to the people: *"Woe be to the shepherds of Israel that do feed themselves! should not the shepherds feed the flocks? Ye eat the fat, and ye clothe you with the wool, ye kill them that are fed: but ye feed not the flock"* (Ezek. 34:2–3). This is evidenced when all of the members are dying spiritually.

You must pay attention to this element because if you are malnourished in the spiritual realm, you will eventually become weak in the natural realm. This is how the anointed whore is developed and sustained. You will be a churched person with no working knowledge and no real power to keep you in the will of God.

Please understand that you are subject to all kinds of defeat if you are not being fed the Word of God. The devil, who is your only enemy, is not concerned with your attending church every week. He is concerned with how much Word is released from your pastor and deposited into your spirit. He will watch you run around and shout until you fall completely out! You can be slain in the spirit, dance to the beat of the drums, and roll all over the floor. But if you have no Word, you will still be defeated.

The Word is the sure weapon that can cause the enemy to flee from you. He knows that he usually wins the fight over one who has no Word. He also knows that he loses with one who has the Word and knows how to apply it.

Jesus was in the wilderness on a forty-day fast when the devil plotted against him with three temptations. With each response, Jesus used the Word of God as his weapon. He clearly could have set the standard of fighting the devil through other means. Yet, Jesus established an example that will lead you into victory every time. He used the Word of God. *"Man shall not live by bread alone, but by every word that proceedeth out of the mouth of God"* (Matt. 4:4).

This is the same example that must be set through your pastor. You will not be victorious over the enemy through weekly poems, personal opinions, daily tips on living, and man-made books. You will be victorious when you are fed the Bible and live by its instructions. Heaven and earth may pass away, but only the Word will remain.

WATERING

"And I will give you pastors according to mine heart, which shall feed you with knowledge and understanding" (Jer. 3:15). It is the Word of God that will save you, heal you, and deliver you. While you are growing in God, your pastor is the connection that drives the Word into your soul. And by the indwelling and operation of the Holy Spirit, the Word is made clear for your spiritual growth, understanding, and development. This is the wa-

tering process. Watering is the element that helps the food (the Word) digest easily and flow to the appropriate places in your life.

As I was maturing in the Lord, God positioned me in a place where I began to see small pieces of my destiny; however, I knew that I would not see the full picture until I connected with a pastor who had the ability to rightly divide the Word of truth (the feeding) and explain it to me in a way that revealed new dimensions of God (the watering). In other words, the watering process was extremely crucial to my understanding of what God had in store for me.

Let me tell you how this process unfolded for me. I was attending a church where I had been a member for many years. After a while, I became stagnated and did not have a mind to grow spiritually. Then, one day I went to a church service and heard a preacher teach on and demonstrate the deliverance power of Jesus Christ. It was as if God had opened my eyes and shown me a new dimension of Himself. I heard and understood biblical truths that I was not familiar with even though I had been in church all of my life. I went back to my church and tried to resume church as usual, but after a while, I knew that I had to make a change. It was time for me to go.

This move did not mean that the former pastor was bad or out of God's will. It only meant that I had to connect with the pastor who was assigned to my next level in God. To be honest, I tried to hang on to the old pastor while trying to connect with the new pastor, but I came to realize that God was repositioning me.

Further, your pastor should be able *to rightly divide the Word of God* in such a way that you have a clear picture of what God is saying, and you are not repeatedly confused. This means that there is an ongoing process that involves the assessment of your spiritual growth as well as a follow-up or measuring tool that allows the shepherd to assess his or her own preparation and delivery.

The shepherd, above anyone else, should be able to give an account of what sheep have learned and are able to master, and whether they are on meat or milk. This is a vulnerable spot because when there is no accountability of growth, members begin to wander away from the fold.

Lack in the watering phase can cause the sheep to wander through the dry mountains (poverty, despair, disobedience) and live without direction. It can also send them to the high hills (being tired, broken, abused, misused, misled) because *"none did search or seek after them"* (Ezek. 34:6). In other words, there was nobody in place to ask where the sheep were, or whether they were digesting the Word through proof of lifestyles.

I can clearly recall a time in my life when I was walking in dry places. Although I had never talked to my pastor about any of my situations, I believe that he sought God for understanding about what was going on with me, and God showed him a glimpse of my soul. My pastor knew that I was slipping away. He knew that I was not digesting the Word and walking in it. One Sunday during this period, my pastor walked up to me and said that he was praying for me and that I should keep returning to God for restoration and mercy. He also began to teach with a stronger conviction about the sin that I was in. In other words, he demonstrated the watering process. This snatched me back!

One of God's complaints to the shepherds of Israel was that they did not provide ongoing care and check-up sessions for the sheep. There was a lack of concern for the development of the members in all areas of their lives. There were no messages or spiritual insight on healthy and prosperous living. There was no training in applying faith or spiritual warfare and certainly no new revelations from God. Ezekiel 34:4 says, *"The weak you have not strengthened, nor have you healed those who were sick, nor bound up the broken, nor brought back what was driven away, nor sought what was lost"* (NKJV). And whenever this happens, the sheep will stray, the little church fights will begin, and some members will even start a church within the church in order to do their own watering!

This is why the pastor must be in the position to teach the Word of God and follow up with watering. If the pastor feeds and waters (and you receive it), you are on your way to living a victorious life in the Lord. If the pastor neglects either, you may be on your way to the hills—not from whence cometh your help but the hills of a backslidden state!

GUIDING

We have walked through the feeding and watering elements of the pastoral role. Now let's look at the guiding element. Guiding is the Word of God being demonstrated through the lifestyle and Word application of your shepherd. This means that you should be able to look at your pastor and see proof of the Word and a revealed pattern that leads you from the enemy's camp to victory through Jesus Christ. This demonstration can only be successful if your pastor lives a life of integrity.

This element has been so underplayed and overlooked that people do not celebrate excellence in those shepherds who are in God's will and are not even shocked when other shepherds fall or are exposed in sin. Church members do not intercede; the community laughs about it, and sometimes the fallen pastor will not even admit the problem or step out of the sin. It is as if we do not realize the seriousness of the pastor's lifestyle. The saints are laughing and the devil is, too. Satan knows that if the pastor goes down, the members are not far behind.

Here is the thought. The guidance element is extremely crucial because many times the pastor's spirit, mannerisms, ideals, behavior, and beliefs are transferred to the members. This transference happens in a spiritual realm and is usually invisible until it fully manifests. Good or bad, if you are truly connected to a pastor, you probably have taken on some of his or her inner make-up.

It will be extremely difficult to be connected with a pastor who teaches and demonstrates tithing, worship, praise, faith, fasting and prayer, and you do not participate. If you are unified with that pastor, you will eventually participate in those teachings and grow as he or she does. This means that your pastor's guidance and demonstration of the Word helped to propel you to a greater level in God.

The flip side of this is that if your pastor demonstrates selfishness, adultery, stealing, or lying, then you may very well take on some of those ways. Again, if you are truly unified with this pastor, you may find yourself being selfish, stealing, and covering up little adulterous affairs. I have seen it happen. You cannot assume that all pastors are yielding to God's will or way of doing things, nor can you ignore or laugh if he or she guides you while living a faulty lifestyle. Their lifestyles are a direct reflection of the level of *active* Word within them and will affect the food that is fed to you on Sunday mornings.

Even for pastors, God communicates with those who have clean hands and a pure heart. Romans 8:7 reminds us that carnality and holiness do not interact successfully. When God comes to reveal the message of life to your pastor, He needs to find a submitted leader who is positioned to hear and release the food to the sheep. He does not need to find a shepherd who is corrupting the sheep by neglecting to study the Word, forfeiting opportunities to demonstrate the Word, or walking in the flesh. He must find a person of integrity!

Although nobody is perfect, at some point your pastor should stand for holiness. When he or she begins to walk in the unadulterated Word of God and God is able to release more, a whole new world opens up for you. This truly makes a difference because the devil will use every tactic possible to destroy you. And if he can use a hypocritical lifestyle from your leader to hinder your growth, then he will.

Pastoral guiding requires holiness, integrity, and consistency. Your pastor should live the same life he or she is preaching. This is serious because you are actually following his or her lead. When Moses was leading the children of Israel out of Egypt, even his small, insignificant actions became life or death signals for the people. Who would have thought that the mere fact of Moses lifting his hands would be seen by the children of Israel as the symbol of strength that kept them moving to victory. His actions were the difference between life and death. And it is still that way today.

PROTECTING

"And they shall no more be a prey to the heathen, neither

shall the beast of the land devour them; but they shall dwell safely, and none shall make them afraid" (Ezek. 34:28). God desires that shepherds maintain the flock with compassion and with a strong arm. He expects them to slay any presumable enemy, keep the sheep from harming one another, and even offer themselves as protection. According to Webster's Dictionary, *protection* is the act of maintaining the status or integrity and covering or shielding one from exposure (being deprived of shelter), injury (pain or harm), and destruction (putting out of existence).

When protection is in the heart and conscience of your pastor, he or she will guard you from exposure to any poison or influence that is designed to steer you away from God. For example, your pastor should not allow any minister or politician to come into the fold and teach inappropriate doctrines, or anyone else to openly confuse or manipulate the sheep. Exposure to such is just as dangerous as physical harm. It only takes one message or one open confession to birth a spiritual disease. And if a spiritual disease infects the congregation, there will be a great risk of spiritual death. This is why the pastors must pay close attention and be ready to respond to any harm that the flock may be exposed to.

Further, protection from spiritual injury or hurt that deeply disrupts your spirit is also significant. Although spiritual injury can come from a variety of sources, it is more likely to occur within the church. Many times ill-hearted members take over certain areas of the church, plant seeds of discord, and deliberately cause harm to other sheep. When this happens, the pastor must have the ability to identify the inside enemy and immediately stop him or her! Even if it is stopped through prayer, it should not be handled with partiality or intentionally ignored.

Finally, the pastor has the great task of using the Word to protect the sheep from destruction. This covering is no longer limited to faith issues, but it now flows from within the walls of the church and even far beyond. The world is so mixed up that the pastor's role now includes protecting one from poverty, AIDS, divorce, bankruptcy, mental relapse, dangerous relationships, addictions, violence, and everything else. Oftentimes, the church is the only nucleus of good information that will ever have an impact on many families. And the pastor must use this power of influence to save the people from the world's influence, from destroying one another, and from self-destructing.

RESTORATION

"Brethren, if a man be overtaken in a fault, ye which are spiritual, restore such an one in the spirit of meekness; considering thyself, lest thou also be tempted" (Gal. 6:1). Finally, let's look at the element that reveals a piece of the shepherd's heart—his or her willingness and ability to restore. *Restoration* is "restoring to an unimpaired or improved condition" (Webster). This is how Jesus

operated in the ministry. His daily walk on this earth demonstrated love, compassion, and restoration. Whenever people encountered Him, whether sick or sad, He always restored them to a better state of being. This is the action and attitude that all shepherds must have.

Like the Good Shepherd, the pastor should always seek opportunities to restore wounded sheep back to a place of righteousness and service. It does not even require a full sermon or counseling session. It could be a two-minute greeting that is spoken through the air of the sanctuary. I have seen some pastors walk into a sanctuary, feel the heaviness of the members, and speak a corporate word of peace upon every member present. They rebuked the enemy's stronghold of oppression and restored the members through one spoken word of faith! That's simple, but that's restoration.

There will be times that you may experience a loss of job, death of a family member, or simply a drop in self-esteem. This is the time that your shepherd has the authority to operate in the spirit of meekness, consider himself or herself, and begin to restore you. When the prodigal son left home, defiled himself and his family's name, then decided to return home, his father restored him and greeted him with a kiss (see Luke 15:10). The father had every right to scold the son and even refuse him of any covering, but he chose to accept him back into the fold and renew his spirit. That's restoration.

Pastoral restoration is a beautiful process because not only can it bring you back into the fold, but it also allows the pastor to enter into a place of submission. It requires pastors to do a review of their lives and realize that the same God that restored them is able to restore you. This is really one of the main elements of Christians that sets us aside from the rest. It defines the cross. Jesus died so that we could be washed, forgiven, and restored back to God.

There are times when the devil might beat you up and leave you for dead, but your pastor, in the spirit of meekness, can restore you back to God. He or she can fully cover and saturate you with the favor and benefits of being on the Lord's side.

Finally, Jesus exemplifies a good shepherd who will sacrifice everything for the sheep:

> *I am the good shepherd: the good shepherd giveth his life for the sheep.*
>
> *But he that is an hireling, and not the shepherd, whose own the sheep are not, seeth the wolf coming, and leaveth the sheep, and fleeth: and the wolf catcheth them, and scattereth the sheep.* (John 10:11–12)

Your shepherd will probably not lay his or her physical life down for you, but he or she should be willing to press in the spiritual realm on your behalf and demonstrate the life before you. The pressing, in itself, will require him or her to lay the life down.

Your pastor has the ability to speak to the dead places of greatness within you and call forth life. He or she has been given the authority to cover you and feed you with the bread of life. You must make sure that you are in the right position and place to hear your words of life from the right shepherd and walk in the fullness that it brings. Remember, spiritual authority is powerful. Let it work for your good.

Dear Father,

We pray for Your leaders and those who operate in spiritual authoritative positions in the Kingdom. Give them the wisdom, knowledge, and ability to move Your people forward according to Your Word.

Help us all to stand against the wiles of the enemy. And grant us your protection and peace.

In Jesus' name,
Amen.

PART III

THE POWER OF RELIGIOUS INFLUENCES—INTERNAL

OFTENTIMES, WE ARE AWARE OF THE EXTERNAL FORCES THAT HAVE THE POWER TO INFLUENCE OUR WALK WITH GOD. HOWEVER, WE MUST ALSO UNDERSTAND THAT THERE ARE INTERNAL FORCES THAT MANIFEST IN THE FORM OF HAVING SELF-DOUBT AND LOW SELF-ESTEEM, HEARING VOICES OF FEAR, HAVING LACK OF GODLY WISDOM, AND BEING TOTALLY NAÏVE THAT ALSO SERVE AS INFLUENCES.

IF YOU ARE NOT CAREFUL, THESE INTERNAL ELEMENTS WILL CAUSE YOU TO STRAY AWAY FROM GOD'S PLAN, MAKE DEADLY DECISIONS, AND SERVE AS YOUR OWN WORST ENEMY.

EIGHT

THE TRAP OF NEEDINESS

"But we have this treasure in earthen vessels,
that the excellency of the power may be
of God, and not of us" (2 Cor. 4:7).

This may sound funny, but I knew something was wrong with me when I would pull up to a convenience store and actually hold a flirtatious conversation with drunk, homeless men who were begging for some "change." Honestly, there was a time in my life that I would actually entertain people who clearly were not suitable for me. In retrospect, I realize that I was at a needy place or in a place of always wanting something from someone else. I only felt good if someone, anyone, approved of me or at least liked me. And of all of the traps that the enemy has, neediness is among the worst.

People who are needy have no clear definition of who they are. They have low self-esteem and will do almost anything to get someone's attention. They will accept verbal and physical abuse, live in filth, become promiscuous, and eventually forfeit their divine destiny.

Until I could define the treasure that was within me, I believed every lie that the devil told me. Not only did I latch on to unhealthy friendships and relationships, but I never fully believed that I could be and have what God said I could.

Now, since I have truly seen some of what God is doing in my life, there is no way that I would purposely entertain anyone who does not line up with what God has shown me. I have no tolerance for foolishness, no tolerance for a career that is beneath me, no tolerance for poverty, no tolerance for wasting time, and no tolerance for ignorance! I strongly believe that once men and women of God fully understand their true purpose and the treasure that lies within, they will never walk in neediness again!

If you are a Christian and are walking in a state of neediness, you must understand that this is a demonic force connecting you to lack, doubt, and insecurity, all of which deny the true power of God. This means that you only believe *some* of the Word. You only believe the portion that helped to pull you out of the world into the confession of Jesus Christ. But you must understand that the Word of God goes further than that. It actually has the power to lift your head and cause you to believe in the treasure that was placed in you from the beginning.

I am reminded of the woman at the well who was married five times, and even after the fifth husband she continued in yet another unhealthy relationship (see John 4). In a way, she was very much like many women today.

First, she greatly desired a true relationship but always seemed to end up with the wrong man. She was married five times. And, although I am not sure what went wrong with the marriages, I can only imagine that the divorce process alone was enough to create neediness. When you have committed yourself to a cause or another person and it fails, there is an automatic challenge in your faith. There is an urge for you to say, *I am* the blame, *I am* not good enough, *I am* not smart enough, or *I am* not pretty enough; and it goes on, and on, and on. And this tearing down process eventually puts you in a needy state of being. Your entire being will believe that you won't be right unless somebody else makes you right.

Secondly, in her relationships, she went from bad to worse—from a state of marriage to a state of shacking up. Although her marriages were not perfect, at least they were marriages, which were honorable and acceptable. But in shacking up, she lost that honor and brought ridicule, embarrassment, and shame upon herself.

Perhaps, she began a relationship with a man that was not hers from a state of desperation and neediness, but this is the state that drives you into deeper debt or into unstable and deadly decisions. It brings about confusion. It keeps you in prayer lines and perpetual counseling sessions with the pastor, never able to pray for yourself and ask God for *your own* deliverance. But I am urging you to rebuke this spirit now!

You have to tell yourself that God did not create you to be used and abused. He did not create you to be a leftover, run-down piece of trash! Neither did He create you to live on the "yes" and "no" of others. But He created you to walk with your head up, make intelligent decisions, with full assurance that you already have within you what it takes to LIVE.

Finally, she knew the Word but had no power to activate it. As she was speaking with Jesus, she was the one who initiated the conversation of the coming Messiah. She was the one who acknowledged that the Christ would be able to set all things in order. This meant that she was actually walking around with the knowledge of the Messiah within her; yet, because she did not have the power of the risen Christ, she failed at prospering in areas of her life, moving from one bad situation to the next.

So, the question is this: why are you walking around with

the full knowledge and power of Jesus Christ but still trying to find fulfillment from somebody or something else? Jesus is all that you need. When the woman at the well actually experienced the power of Jesus, I believe that she stepped out of sorrow, sadness, desperation, and neediness and walked into the excellency of God. The key to doing this is knowing who you are and who He is. When you come into a realization of who you really are in Christ, you will be able to activate the treasure that has been lying dormant within you.

NINE

DON'T BE IGNORANT

"For I do not desire, brethren, that you should be ignorant of this mystery, lest you should be wise in your own opinion"
(Rom. 11:25, NKJV).

"Eye hath not seen, nor ear heard, neither have entered into the heart of man, the things which God hath prepared for them that love Him" (1 Cor. 2:9). Many times we get so excited when we read this scripture or hear someone quote it that we automatically begin to jump, shout, and scream! We are almost out of control because we believe that what God has for us is so big and great that we will never even be able to describe it, believe it, or see it!

We do all of this shouting without even realizing that we actually can see it in the spiritual realm. We *can* see it, it *can* enter into our hearts, and we *can* hear little whispers about what God has for us. It is important that you see it because it is what you will need to survive. This vision will keep you fighting through the report of cancer, fighting although your child is practicing homosexuality, and fighting through bankruptcy. This same vision will keep you standing when you are misunderstood, falling apart, or standing over your parents' grave. It is this confidence in the vision that keeps you moving. You need to know who you are and where you are going.

If you can ever get beyond 1 Corinthians 2:9, you will see that your future does not have to be a mystery. 1 Corinthians 2:10 reads, *"But God has revealed them to us through His Spirit. For the Spirit searches all things, yes, the deep things of God"* (NKJV). This means that God has already released what He has in store for you. It also means that if you have not seen at least some of it, you may need to check yourself. There may be something that is interrupting your ability to receive information in the spiritual realm.

This Word clearly suggests that when you walk in His Spirit, He is able to reveal His plans to you. Your spirit must be ready for communication with the Almighty God. Please understand that God will not bring Himself into a place that does not welcome Him. When He approaches you, He is looking for an image of Himself. If you walk in the flesh, you can rest assured that you will not receive or be able to understand His plans for you.

"But the natural man receiveth not the things of the Spirit of God: for they are foolishness unto him: neither can he know them, because they are spiritually discerned" (1 Cor. 2:14). You have to die daily to your flesh in order to keep the line of communication open. Your mind is incapable of understanding spiritual instructions or insight. The revelations will simply appear to be weird to you.

Think about it. What if God tells you to leave your job and change your profession? In your flesh, you would absolutely think God was making a mistake! On the other hand, if you look at the same situation from spiritual eyes, you will be able to see that God is in control and knows what He is doing. You will know that if God said *Go*, there must be an awesome plan waiting!

This is my testimony. I was a teacher for six years before I walked into my ultimate job, an elementary school principal. After earning my master's degree and stepping out on faith, I was hired as principal at an elementary school in Mississippi. This was an unforgettable time in my life because I now had the opportunity to use my leadership skills to effectively manage a school while expressing my passion for education and children. What a blessing.

I was principal at the school for three years. However, during the third year, God started turning my heart, and I saw myself leaving the school. I remained committed to the children, teachers, and parents, but my spirit became uneasy in that position. I knew that God was preparing me for another place and telling me to resign, quickly. So, with tears in my eyes and courage and dignity in my heart, I resigned. This was the beginning to a crucial, humbling experience of which I will share later in the book.

Nevertheless, when I resigned as principal of that school, no one understood why. People started to wonder if I was really fired, not effective with improving the school's academic standing, or completely foolish. My family was disappointed; and because I did not have another job as expected, at times I began to doubt the decision myself. In fact, the only door that God was opening for me was the opportunity to be a fulltime doctoral student. But through it all, I had to remain obedient and submitted to what God was doing. And it did not look good.

Ultimately, I saw that God was using this experience to provide time for me to write this book, record a CD, earn a doctorate degree, and go through the fire of being called into the ministry! I did not foresee any of this. I was just being obedient.

If I had listened to many people who told me that I needed to work, even if it meant returning to teaching again, I would have delayed what God had for me. I would have been miserable and totally out of His will. In other words, I would have missed out on my real blessing.

The point is you have to be willing to walk away from your perception of what is good for you and be prepared to accept the greater good. Always be spiritually prepared to hear from God and receive what He reveals. This process includes prayer, fasting, and reading and meditating on the Word. If you do this continuously, in God's timing, you will begin to see your purpose.

DON'T TRUST YOURSELF

"For what man knows the things of a man except the spirit of the man which is in him? Even so no one knows the things of God except the Spirit of God" (1 Cor. 2:11, NKJV). Preparing to hear from God is basic. The difficulty comes in when you try to decipher between who or what is really speaking. Who can count the number of times that you have wondered whether God said something, if you said it, or if the devil said it? As we continue through this passage, it will become obvious that it is easy to mistake our spirit for God's voice.

We must understand that sometimes our spirit will reveal and agree with what our flesh really wants to do. And since we are more likely to agree with the flesh, we will talk ourselves into believing that the Holy Spirit is the messenger. The problem with this is that your spirit will probably not represent God's, and you will begin to walk in a lie. You alone will then be responsible for your own demise.

Let's look at how this scenario may possibly unfold. For years, you have admired the popularity of preaching, and now you have actually created the desire to preach. As you have hidden this desire within your soul, it eventually manifests as a revelation from God. Before long, you have heard something say, "Go preach and lead my sheep." And out of obedience to *your own voice*, you will accept your calling, begin a church, devote years of service but will end up preaching to yourself! Eventually, because you are so far from God's will, you will not even want to hear yourself. Now you know something is off if you don't want to hear yourself!

Another example is when there is a strong desire to marry. You envy your friend's marriage, dream about the house and children, and eventually hide this desire so deep within you that it becomes a part of you. Before long, here comes "Mr. Man." He asks you to marry him, and you say, "Yes!" Two months later you walk through the house, look at the man, and ask yourself, "Who in the world is this man?" You see, that is what happens when you trust yourself. You can literally mess *you* up!

The key to hearing God's voice and losing yours is to consistently compare any vision or inner instruction (that you think you hear) with the Word of God. You must also fast, pray, wait for God's peace, and ultimately sacrifice your will. If you are honest with yourself and God, you will be able to understand who is speaking.

Now, I did not mention how to decide whether the devil is speaking because, guess what, we already know. The devil is slick, but most of the time we still know his voice. If what you hear does not line up with the Word, it's usually the voice of the enemy.

WHO'S ADVISING YOU?

1 Corinthians 2:13 reads, *"Which things also we speak, not in the words which man's wisdom teacheth, but which the Holy Ghost teacheth; comparing spiritual things with spiritual."* Once you have positioned yourself in a place of flowing communication with God and He reveals His plans, you may immediately feel the need to share them with others. This feeling is natural and many times necessary. In fact, God wants us to seek wise counsel concerning how to follow through with certain revelation. However, we have to be sure that the counsel is spiritually wise.

Since the beginning of time, the enemy has used the power of influence to pull people away from God's plan. He knows that if he can plant evil within those who are closest to you, then he can get to you. This does not mean that everyone close to you is out to harm you. It only means that you must be sure that those persons of influence fully agree with what God is doing in your life. If you give them the authority to coach you into a blessing, they may also have the authority to delay or deny your blessing. In other words, if you trust them to speak favorable words over your life, you might begin to build a confidence level in them that will influence you to believe *anything* and *everything* they say.

91

Many times these people know you better than anyone, which can make you feel obligated and can cap you with guilt or shame. You may even feel that because they know your past, you owe them something. But when you are trying to believe what God has revealed, you must protect your faith. You should not feel obligated to follow the advice of others. Everyone is not going to understand your position, purpose, or vision. But if they are around you, you need to know their purpose, motives, and hearts towards you. They may touch and agree with you, but ask yourself, "Do they really mean it?"

One clear example is Jairus' story (see Luke 4). Jairus was a ruler of the synagogue. Much like a deacon or trustee, his duties were essential in the daily operation and progression of the local church. One day, Jairus was faced with a life or death situation. His twelve-year-old daughter was gravely ill and was at the point of no recovery. Jairus, having faith in Jesus, quickly left his daughter's side in order to find Him.

Here is the problem: Jairus left his wife and daughter at home with people who appeared to be touching and agreeing for the child's healing. After all, I'm sure that he wanted the saints praying and comforting his wife until he returned.

When Jesus arrived at the house, He found the daughter already dead and people crying over her passing. However, when He said that she was only sleeping, they laughed Him to scorn. This says that while they appeared supportive, they really did not have the kind of faith that Jairus had. This is why you must pray for divine wisdom when you open yourself up to others. Pay close attention to what they are speaking over your life, dissect their words according to the Word of God, and pray that God reveals their inner spirits to you.

As another example, when David slept with Bathsheba and had her husband killed in a battle, God used the prophet Nathan to minister to him. Nathan, because he was already open to the Lord's voice, followed God's instructions when rebuking David. Nathan's approach was so humble and wise that David was moved to repent and felt sorrowful for what he had done. This is the type of counsel that God wants us to listen to, counsel that moves you toward God's will.

Your future is so powerful in the Kingdom that your inner circle of counsel must see you as God sees you. Your circle cannot be a group of people that walk after the flesh. How will they know what to say to you when you are tempted to fall back into sin? What scriptures will they use? Will they fast and pray with you when it's time for you to minister? Can they warn you when danger is approaching? If they are walking in the flesh, the answer is "No." They may be nice, trustworthy, and ready to touch and agree. But the fact is that they cannot walk in the Spirit and in the flesh at the same time.

Do not allow anybody to detour you with opinions that are made in the flesh. You must remember that the Holy Spirit is the ultimate teacher who will share the things of God with those who have the Spirit of God in them. Yes, He is looking for Himself.

TEN

SEEN BUT NOT ACKNOWLEDGED

"For the gifts and the calling of God are
irrevocable" (Rom. 11:29, NKJV).

Not only do you have to make sure that those who are around you are good for you, but you also have to make sure that you are not depending on them for validation. Those whom you expect to offer advice and acknowledge what God is doing through you may not actually be there to do it. Who knows why? They could be jealous, busy, or simply not ready to deal with your next level. And if you really need them to validate you, the enemy is going to get the best of you.

Please understand that people recognize the gift in you. They may not acknowledge you or call you forward to exercise your gift, but trust me, they see you.

So, this is how the enemy works it. He makes you believe

that your gift is not valid until you are called out by your pastor, your friends, your boss, your family, or any other respected person in your life causing you to be frustrated with the gift or to simply throw it away. But you must not be fooled by this. You have to believe in what God showed you and not depend on how soon or if you will ever be publicly acknowledged.

If you notice, as your gift and calling become more evident, those who you want to acknowledge it will probably talk about everything else other than your spiritual promotion. Seriously, you can be caught up in the middle of the air—in the middle of church service—spinning around on a big white cloud, and after church your best friend might say, "Girl, what are we eating today?" And you are thinking, "Oh, my goodness! I know she saw me floating and spinning in the air! Why is she talking about food?" And what happens is that you will eventually think your gift or calling is not there or is not good enough to be recognized.

I clearly remember those times when God was calling me into the ministry, and I was ministering under a very powerful and unusual anointing and nobody said anything. I mean the church was "torn-up," but there were no verbal responses or confirmations. Nothing. It was as if I never went to church. And it was a long time before this transformation was acknowledged. Sure, people told me that I did well, or they were blessed by my ministry. But I am not talking about them. I am talking about the prophets or those who are really connected to God and have the discernment to see Him growing in a person.

During this time of silence, the devil told me to "go sit down." And I almost did. But the devil is a lie! I made it through. I was strong enough to get through the many times that I felt bad when those who could have been cultivating and supporting me were not. And I still feel bad for people who really believe they need the affirmation and do not make it through this period. I have seen people leave the church and leave God just because someone did not acknowledge their gift or calling. Oh, my goodness! It is such a trick of the enemy.

Saints, you have to understand that God will send you mentors and lifters when it is time. Until then, you must encourage yourself. You have to take the initiative to cultivate your gift through the Word and watch God give the increase. You cannot live on what you *think* somebody should be telling you. If you have an encourager—great! But by all means, this factor must not be allowed to make you sit down on your gifts.

When I began to notice that I was being called into the ministry, I did not understand what was happening to me. I had this overwhelming draw to the cross, I began to view the worship service differently, and I began to really pay attention to the preached Word of God. As the choir director at my church, not only would I teach songs during rehearsals, but I felt a strong desire to explain the meaning of the songs.

I also began to see the church service in a different way. I saw it as an opportunity to be in the presence of God instead of an opportunity to be in the usual order of service. As time went on, I began to understand what was happening. My duties as a praise and worship leader were slowly turning into teaching and speaking the Word.

The point is that I was in a strange place, and I needed someone who had experienced or could identify with the place I was in to confirm what was happening. Since this place was unfamiliar, and nobody helped me, I began to question God and wonder why He was moving me this way and not explaining. Therefore, as I began to go higher in the spirit, I also felt naked.

I felt naked because I was out of place. I felt like I was the only one who wanted to linger in the presence of God beyond the church program. I thought I was the only one who wanted to worship a little longer and not rush into church announcements. I felt crazy. In fact, there were many times when I had to beg God not to let me feel that burning within my spirit because I knew that I had to keep directing the choir, and the inner burning might interrupt the flow of the service. I'm telling you, this was something!

This turning point was very strange. There were times when I would find myself at church in body only, but in the spiritual realm I was at the feet of God. I am telling you, people thought

I was crazy. They started thinking that just because I "saw the light" doesn't mean they had to see it. At this point, I badly needed some mentors!

Fortunately, after the Lord allowed me to understand some changes within myself, He sent three preachers to me. (I told you that He would send someone in His timing.) As I stood and looked at them, I almost fell out because I had just asked God to send somebody to me to explain what I was experiencing. But when they showed up, it really scared me!

They were all members of my church and were waiting for me after Bible study one night. One of them began to tell me that they could see that God was doing a new thing in me, and the others joined in. They began to say that they could see God moving me beyond just directing the choir and singing. They said that God was calling me out, getting me ready, sending me through, washing me, and cleaning me up so that I could be used to call others out. Soon after that, other people began to see what God was doing with me, and they called it forth as well.

I am saying this to help you understand that you must not run away because you are seen but not acknowledged. God knows when to bring you forth and when to send mentors or prophets to you. Until that happens, keep seeking God through His Word and wait. Do not give in to the enemy. Stay in the fight and keep glorifying God.

Dear Father,

We thank You for revealing the enemy that comes as an angel of light. We acknowledge that we have not been attentive enough to our internal influences that reveal our own uncertainties and weaknesses. But in Your promise to have mercy, we pray that You guide us and teach us to guard our own minds and hearts as we walk in Your will.

Provide for us the covering that only You can give and heal our internal infirmities. We pray for opportunities to prove our new way of thinking and living.

In Jesus' name,
Amen.

PART IV

PLANTING THE VISION

AS GOD BEGINS TO REVEAL HIS PLAN FOR YOU, YOU WILL FIND THAT THERE MAY BE A SEASON OF DOWNTIME. DURING THIS TIME, WHICH I CALL THE DARKROOM, YOU WILL SEE JUST HOW STRONGLY YOUR PERSONAL WILL CAN FIGHT AGAINST YOUR DIVINE DESTINY.

THIS SECTION REVEALS A RAW, UNCUT VIEW OF WHAT CAN HAPPEN AS GOD REVEALS YOUR PURPOSE IN THE KINGDOM. IT UNCOVERS THE STRENGTH OF THE ENEMY THAT LIVES IN YOUR MIND AS WELL AS THE SIGNIFICANCE OF TOTAL SUBMISSION TO GOD.

ELEVEN

MY DARKROOM

"And the Lord said unto Moses, Stretch out thine hand toward heaven,
that there may be darkness over the land of Egypt, even darkness which
may be felt" (Exod. 10:21).

There is a room that is so black that you believe the darkness is tangible. Your head spins in doubt and fear, and your heart is filled with sorrow. Your body is so heavy with depression that you can hardly lift your legs out of bed. And if you make it out of bed, each additional step is filled with misery and pain. This is the room that you are in when God is breaking, purging, and preparing you to walk in His plan for you. This was my darkroom.

This period in my life began after I resigned as principal of the elementary school. This new way of living became an extremely humbling experience for me. You must understand that I had never faced the idea of being "without." From the time I earned my first degree until the time of my resignation as principal, I had never seen a rough financial day. In fact, "I had it made." I was independent, drove a Mercedes Benz E320, traveled at my own will, and spent my own money. Life was great.

Even when I resigned and left the city where the school was, I believed that I was still in good condition because I had a plan. I planned to move back to Jackson, find another job as an administrator, enroll in a doctoral program, continue my duties at the church, and spend time with my family and cute little boyfriend. Yes, I had it all mapped out.

Then, the horror began. God closed all doors to a job, and He started separating me from everything that was comfortable and familiar. It felt as if I was forced to shut myself in my bedroom, remain in the dark, and cry all day and night. I had no desire to communicate with friends, family, church people, or anyone else. Eventually, I refused to see anyone or talk with anyone on the phone. I told all of my friends that I needed them to leave me alone for a while and just pray. It seemed as if I was slowly sinking into serious depression.

There were times when I would lie in bed and look up towards heaven, but the tears were so thick that I could not see the ceiling. I could only feel the tears rolling down either side of my face. Every now and then, I tried to whisper a prayer, but I did not have the strength, nor did I believe that God could hear me. To be honest, there were even times when I doubted God's very existence.

From time to time, my mother would come in the room and ask me to get up and get some air. But I could not. All I could do was cry and wonder what was happening to me. Finally, when I went as low as I could go and experienced a series of storms, God spoke. In a sweet and soft but firm manner, God told me that He was going to use me as a mouthpiece to gain souls for the Kingdom.

Now let me interrupt this testimony to say that I believe that when God gets ready to send you a strong message concerning His will for you, He will put you in a place where you can hear only His voice. You may not have to experience my darkroom, but your spirit and soul will at least be vulnerable enough to hear God's plans. By the time I heard God speak to me, I was so weak until I had no choice but to hear Him. I did not have the mind or the strength to trust myself or listen to anyone else.

You cannot be dismayed when trouble hits your life, or when your normal living arrangements and relationships become shuffled or disturbed. You must remember that some trouble, especially the kind that just pops up out of the blue, may be the perfect condition for God to speak to you. Now I can hear some of you saying, "I'm not claiming trouble just so that I can go higher in

God!" You are right. You should not claim trouble. I am simply saying that if trouble comes, don't try to commit suicide! Make the best of it. Be still and listen for the small, still voice of God.

In 1 Kings, chapter 19, when Elijah was running from Jezebel, he found himself hiding in a cave (his darkroom). As he was there, God commanded him to come out of the cave and ordered him to a place where he would be exposed to a series of storms. As Elijah witnessed strong winds, an enormous earthquake, and a great fire, I am sure he thought that God would reveal Himself in those storms. But, actually, Elijah did not hear from God until all of the storms ceased. This says that before God gets ready to further instruct you, you may experience some storms.

God can use a crucial situation to get your full attention, and then He will speak when you are broken and ready to receive instruction. In other words, He is the voice that you hear when you have settled yourself enough to hear.

Indeed, after the storms got Elijah's attention, he was able to receive God's plan. Saints, this is all that storms and darkrooms are allowed to do. They get your attention and push you into activating the Word and walking in God's will.

Consider another point. As I was in my darkroom and needing to hear from God, I was totally secluded from outside influences. I did not know it then, but now I understand that this room was so vulnerable that I could not afford to be influenced either by those who could harm me or those who really loved me and just wanted to help. This was an open season for the enemy, and any advice could have triggered the wrong move.

You must understand that in this season of your life, you are actually fighting off nervous breakdowns, voices of suicide, and any other form of self-destruction. This is very serious; therefore, you must let God be in full control.

As you experience this transition, you must have the courage to demand personal space and time to understand what is happening to you. Bring yourself and your actions to a settled place and wait for the vision and whispers of God.

TWELVE

THE VISION THAT CHANGED ME

"I, Daniel, was grieved in my spirit within my body, and the visions of my head troubled me" (Dan. 7:15, NKJV).

As I stated earlier, I heard the voice of the Lord calling me to a more prominent position in the Kingdom; but since I was still in the darkroom, I was experiencing doubt, low self-esteem, and self-pity. Therefore, I did not feel that I was equipped to deliver a message to anyone. On top of that, I began to think, "How could God have the audacity to ask me to do something for Him? After all, He allowed me to go through this much pain and get this bad off!" So, I began a journey of rejecting the call.

I did not want to do anything for God! I was already bitter about losing my lifestyle. And certainly, I was not willing to give it all up for people I did not know. I wanted to stay just like I was.

Just like I was! And for days after I heard God's call into the ministry, I remained in that same rebellious state.

Then, one day as I was lying in bed, God, in a vision, showed me an auditorium filled with people who were hurting and needing to hear about Jesus Christ. I saw their faces. I saw their bodies. I saw their issues. They were real people with real life or death circumstances. There were little girls who had been molested, little boys who were addicted to drugs, grown men who were physically abusive, and grown women who were being emotionally and physically abused. I saw every kind of person from every walk of life. They were all looking at me and hanging on to every word that was coming out of my mouth. They knew that in those words was their last hope.

God then told me that I had to step out of that vision and actually stand on that platform to tell people about Jesus. At this point, I was not thrilled at all. The anxiety of standing and delivering a message was overwhelming, and I was not about to change my life in this way. So, in a matter of seconds, I tried to get out of it.

But later in that hour, I began to visualize those same people dying. I saw them all in black and knew they were dying because I refused to tell them about Jesus. This forced me into a place of grief. Over the course of several weeks, I felt like I was attending a funeral for each of them. Many times, I would yell out and try to get that heavy feeling out of my mind and out of my spirit. It did not leave.

And although I felt sorry for those people, I still did not want to sacrifice my life for them. I wanted to keep working and keep directing the choir. I wanted to just be me, with no interruptions. In other words, my personal will for my life was fighting to win over God's will. I was on my way to *Tarshish* (a place of escape), traveling in a fish. Jonah called it the *belly of hell*.

THIRTEEN

THE BELLY OF HELL

"Now the Lord had prepared a great fish to swallow up Jonah. And Jonah was in the belly of the fish three days and three nights" (Jon.1:17).

As you are trying to deal with a call on your life, you may find yourself asking for more confirmations. And as time passes, God will answer that prayer. In my case, God sent me two strong confirmations.

The first confirmation came from a preacher who lived in Wilmington, North Carolina. I first met him at a conference in Florida. A few years later, I traveled to California with my pastor and church choir to sing at a national conference held by my church denomination. There we were reunited. After my returning home to Jackson, we spoke over the phone and during that conversation he asked, "Are you preaching?" I simply responded, "No."

Then he said, "Lisa, it's there, and you'd better deal with the call that is on your life."

The second confirmation came from a preacher who lived in Alabama and was guest speaker for a women's conference at my church. I hardly knew her, but she gave me the same prophecy as the other preacher. During the conference, she did an altar call. And as I stood before her, she laid her hands on me and whispered, "The same thing I am doing to you, you will be doing to others."

"Oh, Lord," I thought, "God is getting serious. He's sending out the prophets. He's not playing anymore!" I became seriously nervous. I stood at the altar a few more minutes and returned to my seat. I was anxious to leave church and get away quickly.

That night, I drove around the city of Jackson and tried to make sense of it all. I came to realize that God was not saying anything to me that did not deal with His purpose and my appointment. There was no place to run or hide. No doubt, I was in the belly of hell. And to those of you who are in this spot, watch out for some extreme behavior!

First, let's look at the *extremely good behavior*: you will begin to sit in church services and see situations that can be better with your intervention. You may even find yourself wanting to help someone less fortunate. You may supply clothes to the Red Cross or offer your specialized services for free. You begin to give one or two dollars to the homeless person you see waiting at the traffic light or pray with friends who are getting weak. You offer advice to people in messed up relationships. You do all of this and still there is no fulfillment.

Then comes the *extremely bad behavior*: you don't want to go to church. You are certainly tired of sermons. You begin to do things that represented your life before you were saved. You date unsaved people, start drinking before bed, start cussing people out, start reading books during church service, start gossiping, start showing up late and hanging out with thugs, start gaining weight, and start paying your bills late. I am telling you, it can get weird.

When there is a call on your life and a specific assignment for you, no charity commitment can take its place. You do all of this and *still* have to face it. God has called you out! Jonah's journey is not easy. You may run but you can't hide. You can bargain with God, but He is not listening. You will have to stay there and make a conscious decision to surrender to His will. By no means is this easy. In fact, I am willing to say that if it seems easy, you may be hearing the wrong thing. At least for me, the process was a true Jonah, belly of hell, experience!

This experience feels like a burden that weighs on you like heavy iron. The iron is the sorrow of the people who are crying out for help coupled with your rebellion. It is like walking around with thousands of bricks on your shoulder. Above all, you wish that you could escape your mind. And you know that's not possible.

During this period, the devil works overtime to get you to denounce what God has called you. He will show you failing at your vision, struggling to survive financially, or even having to fight with people in order to make the vision stay alive. You will see yourself giving up and becoming disconnected from your purpose. Ultimately, if you do not come out of this journey with the fish, you will find yourself at the mercy of the enemy. You do not want that to happen.

I really believe that you determine how long you are in the belly of hell. Jonah stayed there until he decided to surrender. God did not command the fish to release Jonah until after Jonah's prayer of submission and commitment. You have to make a decision to die to yourself and realize that nothing you do outside of God's appointment will prosper. It may look like it is prospering but believe me, it's not. Jonah said in his prayer that when his soul fainted within him, he remembered the Lord. He called out to Him and made a vow that he would sacrifice his will with thanksgiving (see Jon. 2:1–10). And this is what you must do—you must completely surrender and forsake everything that has the potential to hold you back.

Whatever your call is, you have to answer it. Do not force God to make adjustments to your life before you become obedient. Remember, God is not only calling you into your destiny, but He is also calling you out of a state of disobedience. He's enabling you to transition from a life of double standards to an honest and complete life of integrity in Him.

FOURTEEN

Go!

*"Ye shall not need to fight in this battle: set yourselves, stand
ye still, and see the salvation of the Lord with you, O Judah
and Jerusalem: fear not, nor be dismayed; to morrow go out against
them: for the Lord will be with you" (2 Chron. 20:17).*

Guess what happens when you choose to listen and submit
to God? God speaks! Jonah said to God:

> *I am cast out of thy sight; yet I will look again toward
> thy holy temple.*
>
> *The waters compassed me about, even to the soul: the
> depth closed me round about, the weeds were wrapped
> about my head.*
>
> *I went down to the bottom of the mountains; the earth*

with her bars was about me for ever: yet hast thou brought up my life from corruption, O Lord my God. (Jon. 2:4–6)

In response, *"the Lord spake unto the fish, and it vomited out Jonah upon the dry land"* (Jon. 2:10). When Jonah surrendered, God immediately commanded the fish to release him on dry land. In other words, He said, "Let Jonah go and place him on safe ground!"

When you are set free, you do not have to worry about the waters overtaking you. You no longer have to worry about weeds and unfamiliar objects that surround you as you sleep. You do not have to worry about the bars of hell closing on you in a dark place of condemnation and death.

God said, "Put him on dry land so that he can do what I asked him to do. Let him out!" Doesn't that sound good? Let him out!

When God says that, He means that.

He speaks to the whole hellacious situation.

He speaks to the trouble, the trials, and the fainted soul.

Wow!

The thought of God saying, "Let Lisa out!" is incredible!

Yes, let me out! I need to get out! Open your mouth and let me out! Let me out! Whew, that's in my spirit!

Let me out, depression. Let me out, lack.

Let me out, man. Let me out, phony religion.

Let me out, confusion. Let me out, worry.

Let me out, pride. Let me out, doubt. Let me out and put me on dry land. Thanks for the ride, but I've got to go.

Thanks for being my friend during my time in the belly of hell, but I've got to go. Thanks for listening to me complain, but now, I've got to go. Thanks for loaning me money, but now, I've got to go. Saints, when it's time to go, don't feel bad. Go! Give thanks to the people who were in that season with you, but go. Tell them you appreciate them, you love them, you will never forget what they did, but go.

Do not look back. Pay any debt that you owe, but go. Mend all broken relationships and go. Close every situation that is open and go! Find everybody that was there with you, seal it off, and go. Apologize for any offenses you may have committed, give back any clothes you borrowed, and go. Step on dry land and begin that good work that God has begun in you *"being confident of this very thing, that He who has begun a good work in you will complete it until the day of Jesus Christ"* (Phil. 1:6, NKJV).

Dear Father,

We pray that You will forgive us for those times when we did not trust You. We now realize that the darkrooms have been a major part in our lives, and that You did not lose control during those times.

Help us to hear Your assignments and move swiftly to do Your work. As we have decided to follow You, we ask that You help us sever the connection with anything that does not represent You.

In Jesus' name,
Amen.

PART V

DELIVERANCE

IT IS TIME FOR CHRISTIANS TO UNDERSTAND THAT MAKING A QUICK DECISION TO STOP COMMITTING A SIN DOES NOT NECESSARILY MEAN THAT THE ROOT OF THE SIN IS DESTROYED. THIS IS EVIDENT WHEN ONE BECOMES ENTANGLED AGAIN WITH OLD BONDAGE.

THIS SECTION PUSHES YOU TO TRUST THE REPENTANCE PROCESS. IT WILL GUIDE YOU THROUGH A SERIES OF SEASONS THAT LEAD YOU TO TRUE DELIVERANCE. BE PREPARED TO STAND FACE-TO-FACE WITH YOUR "INNER MAN" AS WELL AS FIND OUT WHY YOU MAY BE CREATING AND SUSTAINING YOUR OWN TRAPS AND ENTANGLEMENTS.

FIFTEEN

THE FOUNDATION

"Help us, O God of our salvation, for the glory of
thy name: and deliver us, and purge away our sins,
for thy name's sake" (Ps. 79:9).

One of the most horrible feelings is to be trapped in a place of danger without the ability to even ask for help. I can recall times when I was having a nightmare, and I was trying to open my mouth and scream for help. But nothing happened. I could not open my mouth. In the dream, I could see myself only seconds away from death. I'm telling you, it was a suffocating feeling. However, moments before I was to be harmed, I woke up! It was as if God saw me struggling to live, and He stepped in to save me from dying. In other words, He delivered me!

Sometimes, you can be so deep in harm's way that you feel

yourself trying to get out, but you cannot open your mouth. You see the domestic violence. You see the danger of promiscuity. You see the physical effects of drugs. Still, you can't get your mouth open to ask for help. But thank God, He sees the heart that is begging for help, and He wakes you up! God Himself steps in and delivers you.

Deliverance means being rescued from danger. It is being unchained from any ungodly practices, which severely bind you. Deliverance is a spiritual act that is manifested in a change of heart, a change of mind, and a change of behavior. Although it can be explained through various patterns, the basis of any deliverance process includes salvation (belief in Jesus Christ) and repentance, faith in the Word of God, and faith in the power of the blood of Jesus Christ. When this foundation is laid, and you are filled with and led by the Holy Spirit, deliverance can take place. This entire process takes commitment and strength that can only come from God.

DELIVERANCE THROUGH SALVATION AND REPENTANCE

"For it is impossible for those who were once enlightened, and have tasted of the heavenly gift, and were made partakers of the Holy Ghost, and have tasted the good word of God, and the

powers of the world to come, If they shall fall away, to renew them again unto repentance; seeing they crucify to themselves the Son of God afresh, and put him to an open shame" (Heb. 6:4–6).

Before we move through this section of deliverance through salvation and repentance, I know many of you are saying that you are already saved. However, we must also understand that salvation is not just a onetime confession and then returning to an old lifestyle. And repentance is not merely asking God to forgive you.

To be saved is to confess your belief in the Lord Jesus Christ and believe in your heart that God raised Him from the dead (see Rom. 10:9). Now, that is simple. But it does not end there. Once you confess that Jesus is the risen Savior who was given as a ransom for you, your actions and mindset have to be transformed to that belief. And repentance is when you go before God, confess the sin, and use all of the resources that God has made available to stay away from that sin forever. Repentance, therefore, is when you turn away from that act of sin.

When you were called out of the world, you were expected to walk in the newness of Jesus Christ. In other words, you were not called out of the darkness to return to it again. You do not have the right to be saved and bound at the same time. This is offensive towards the Holy Spirit, and it frustrates the entire purpose of Jesus' death and resurrection.

In essence, salvation and repentance bring about freedom, cleanliness, righteousness, and holiness. Your actions and thinking have to be aligned to this new way of living. So, then, salvation does not end at confession. Nor does repentance end at recognition of the sin. They are both manifested in a new way of living!

Ephesians 2:10 says that we are God's workmanship. And we know that God did not make and mold us to be drug addicts, homosexuals, adulterers, fornicators, murderers, gossipers, liars, and haters. He saved us through Christ Jesus unto good works. He designed us to walk in the power of His resurrection. If we walk in the power of the resurrection, we automatically have the authority to be delivered!

DELIVERANCE THROUGH THE WORD OF GOD

Once you have made the decision to surrender and move towards walking in God's will for you, your next step will be a face-to-face encounter with yourself. This season of deliverance is when the Holy Spirit begins to uncover the hidden side of you all for the purpose of renewing your mind, body, and soul. This is when you will activate the Word of God as your cleansing tool.

When I went through this phase, God pulled the covers back and up jumped selfishness, pride, jealousy, doubt, and inse-curity, just to name a few. Seeing myself in this way literally felt like someone was scraping me inside out. I could not believe what

I saw! It was a rough and scary sight, but I knew I had to let it run its full course.

It was so weird to me that I did not know where to begin my prayers. And when I got tired of seeing what was hiding in me, I began to sleep all day and eat all night. I also began to play games and try to bribe God. Sometimes, I would even be so angry at God until I found myself forgiving Him. I would say, "God, I know You love me, so I forgive You for doing this." I am telling you, this process of deliverance can be compared to a washing machine cycle. You are literally maneuvered back and forth, around and around, until you are clean!

As time went on, I started dealing with those issues. I took myself through a process that included fasting for a few hours a day. During the fast, I acknowledged the iniquity that was shown to me, located it in the Bible, and used the scriptures to get rid of it.

For example, when I saw a spirit of pride within me, I searched the scriptures to find every word that dealt with pride. Once I located the scriptures, I began to repeatedly speak them and embed them into my heart. I had to be vigilant because the pride had taken root into my spirit and was cleverly disguised as mere confidence. With this in mind, my prayers began to look like this:

Dear Father,

Proverbs 16:18–19 says that *"pride goeth before*

destruction, and an haughty spirit before a fall. Better it is to be of an humble spirit with the lowly, than to divide the spoil with the proud." And Proverbs 16:5–7 says that *"every one that is proud in heart is an abomination to the Lord: though hand join in hand, he shall not be unpunished. By mercy and truth iniquity is purged: and by the fear of the Lord men depart from evil."* So, Lord, with the blood of Jesus, wash pride out of my heart. Purge me with mercy and truth and help me to depart from evil. I will not be destroyed because of this pride, and I will walk in humble submission. I declare that I am free of pride, and that it will never live in my mind or my heart again.

In Jesus' name,

Amen.

This is the type of prayer that sets you free. When the Lord exposes the real you, it must be fearlessly driven out with the Word and the blood of Jesus. Yes, your prayer has to grow up! You have to move from, "Lord, when it's all over, receive me in your Kingdom" to "Lord, if you don't get this hell out of me, I am not going to make it to your Kingdom!" You have to get real!

As I continued with the steps of fasting and confessing the Word to become clean, I began making some adjustments. Day by day, I started dropping off some of the works of the flesh and producing the fruits of the Holy Spirit (see Gal. 5). This process went on for months until I became more comfortable in this place of total submission.

I can hear you say, "Months?" Yes, several months. If I'm not mistaken, it was eighteen months! You must understand that it takes time and hard work to get years of negative influences out of you. You may stop committing the very act of the sin, but driving that spirit all the way out is a different degree of work. You have to activate the Word of God and the blood of Jesus. This takes spiritual persistence and diligence.

DELIVERANCE THROUGH THE BLOOD

"But now in Christ Jesus ye who sometimes were far off are made nigh by the blood of Christ" (Eph. 2:13). I am certain that if we really understood the power of the blood of Jesus Christ, we would not remain entangled in the enemy's bondage. This scripture reminds us that no matter how messed up we are, no matter how hooked we are, no matter how stupid and caught up we are, the blood of Jesus can clean us up and bring us back to God.

"For the life of the flesh is in the blood: and I have given it to you upon the altar to make an atonement for your souls: for it is the blood that maketh an atonement for the soul" (Lev. 17:11). The blood is a critical element because from the beginning God has required a blood sacrifice for atonement, that is, the taking away of

sins.

"And almost all things are by the law purged with blood; and without shedding of blood is no remission" (Heb. 9:22). In the Old Testament, the blood of animals was required to purify the people that God might dwell among them. However, the blood of animals is no longer acceptable. We now understand that in order for us to be reconciled unto God, the only blood that is acceptable is that of Jesus Christ.

As I am presenting the blood of Jesus as a part of the foundation for deliverance, I must first address what it will *not* do. The blood of Jesus will not run you down, overpower you, and snatch you away from your sins. It does not fight with you in order to persuade you to become clean. The blood of Jesus should be seen as an active flow of power that will work for you when you step into it.

Once you have accepted Jesus into your life and have offered yourself as a living sacrifice, the blood can then be activated to wash away your sins and purge your mind. To be purged means to be rid of or made free from anything that is defiled. *"How much more shall the blood of Christ, who through the eternal Spirit offered himself without spot to God, purge your conscience from dead works to serve the living God?"* (Heb. 9:14).

When the blood purges your conscience, it completely rids it of anything defiled. Once applied, its power cannot be overthrown by any evil force, nor can it leave any place unclean. This means that the blood is so effective that you will not even have a mind to remain in that state of sin. Your thought patterns will be different and eventually your emotions and desires will fall into order. You will absolutely have the power to walk away from what you used to do!

"Wherefore Jesus also, that he might sanctify the people with his own blood" (Heb. 13:12). I have been so washed from some of my dead works to the point that when I think about them, I know without doubt, that I will not step back into them. Now I can hear someone saying, "Never say never." And I still say that I will never do some of what I used to do. People who use caution when speaking of deliverance are probably people who have not been washed in the blood. They simply chose to stop committing the sin.

Please understand that some sin can be so painful that you may automatically turn away from it. However, whenever the hurt heals, and a little time has passed, you may find yourself falling into it again. This is what we call "slipping." For example, if you find yourself gambling again, the first thing you will say to yourself and to God is, "Lord, forgive me. I slipped." When, actually, that sin or spirit of bondage was never washed completely out. You, probably, just stopped gambling because you got caught or lost your house! There is a huge difference in stopping and being delivered by the blood.

When you are truly washed of an iniquity, it is gone. You will be able to stand toe-to-toe with that sin and not give in to it. Don't let the enemy trick you; "slipping" is not acceptable. It's a sign that you need to be washed for real!

Finally, you have to believe that the blood of Jesus can clean your conscience and wash away your sins. And just a reminder—there is no sin or bondage that the blood of Jesus cannot wash away. Thank God! *"But now once in the end of the world hath he appeared to put away sin by the sacrifice of himself"* (Heb. 9:26).

SIXTEEN

SEASONS OF DELIVERANCE

"Daniel answered and said, Blessed be the name of God for
ever and ever: for wisdom and might are his: And he changeth the times
and the seasons: he removeth kings, and setteth
up kings: he giveth wisdom unto the wise,
and knowledge to them that know understanding:
He revealeth the deep and secret things:
he knoweth what is in the darkness, and the light
dwelleth with him" (Dan. 2:20–22).

As I applied the foundational tools for deliverance (salvation, repentance, the Word, and the blood), the Holy Spirit urged me to go deeper. I was encouraged to dig and search for the foundation of my sins and bad choices. I needed to find out why I would intentionally cause harm to myself. And, as I discovered some of the roots, I realized that I was moving through a whole other process, which I call *seasons of deliverance.* Seasons of deliverance are: discovering the core, confronting the core, developing trust, facing the shame, experiencing intimacy and vulnerability, and being set free.

Brothers and sisters, this is an entirely different journey that requires you to pray for mental stability. Whenever you move through extremely vulnerable phases, you must be prepared to encounter events that may bring tears and stir up all other emotions and uneasiness. Doubt and self-pity attempt to overtake your mind and will even push you to end the deliverance process. But you must stand strong against the enemy by continuously applying the foundational tools and remaining focused on being set free.

DISCOVERING THE CORE, OR "WHERE DID IT COME FROM?"

A core represents the heart of a matter, both present and past. This is exactly why the *Church Fights* section was included in this book. Even though it is hard for us to hear, we must understand that we cannot detach ourselves from our past. The harsh reality is that our past, good or bad, is *our* past. It is an eternal part of our life story. The key to moving beyond or gaining victory over your past is using it to promote you to higher ground. This is done when you gather the information and learn as much as you can so that you do not repeat any self-violation, or allow it to manipulate your future.

Remember the self-destructive relationships from the *Happy Faults* section? Well, here's the connection. One of the areas of which I needed deliverance was in my relationships with men, both intimate and social.

I was a girl who became a woman that clearly had a defect when it was time to make good relationship selections. The deciding factor for me was mostly biased. It was based on an internal void that was created through my relationship with my father. My father was my prize. I absolutely adored every strand of his wavy, coarse hair. In fact, we loved each other so much that I am certain he would have given his life for me.

There was only one problem: because my parents were divorced, I did not get enough time with him. I saw him on the weekends and other special occasions. But every time I left him, I felt robbed, robbed of love and robbed of protection. I knew he was there, but I could not touch him. And, because of the void, I found replacements and made several decisions based on that emptiness. This influenced who I admired, who I hated, who I trusted, who I allowed into my heart, and the longevity of my relationships. These replacements, good or bad, were fake and many times potentially harmful. They only filled a spot in my imagination. They never really filled the void, nor did they make the situation better. What eventually happened is that, as I piled on more and more replacements, I grew deeper and deeper in bondage. Ultimately, this deficiency became a part of me even as an anointed vessel.

The trick is that I did not even know that I was seeking replacements. To be honest, I did not know that I had a void. The replacements just became a part of my behavior. However, as I began to seek God for deliverance in this area, this was the part that had to be scraped up and magnified. Had I never faced this root with my father, I would never have been able to look at my replacements and walk away from them for good.

Once this connection was made, I had to expose this root and make it available to the foundational tools of deliverance. The Word of God and the blood of Jesus had to be applied to the place where the bondage began.

Saints, this is what opens your understanding and brings healing to your soul. Burying it is not the answer. All of it has to be made available. Remember, *"we know that all things work together for good to them that love God, to them who are the called according to his purpose"* (Rom. 8:28). That's you! Let it *all*, even your roots, work for your good.

CONFRONTING THE CORE

When the core of the matter has been discovered, the next

step is to confront it. In this season, you will literally disrupt and disturb the nucleus of what has you bound. For example, as I went a little deeper in my process of deliverance, I had to confront a physical offense that took place over 15 years ago and had the potential to destroy me for the rest of my life.

When I was a young girl, I was violated by an older male family acquaintance. Although I was not raped, for years, as a result of the incident, I was deeply wounded and overtaken with feelings of guilt, shame, confusion, and neglect. Yet, I knew that if I were to ever recover, I had to confront it. So, as an adult, I gathered my thoughts, dealt with each minute of that violation, and found the strength to strongly confront it.

I contacted those whom I felt were partially responsible and expressed the pain and hurt that was buried within me. More importantly, I released and forgave my offender. I did not call him or hunt him down. But I did release him, which also set me free from those things that had kept me bound for years.

This is what you must do with any dark issues of your life—you must confront them. How can you be free from something that you do not confront? Believe it or not, the devil's purpose of my experience was to steal, kill, and destroy me. He wanted me to feel unworthy of a healthy and respectful relationship. He could have even planted a seed of promiscuity and hatred against all men. His plans for my destruction were endless. That is why it had to be confronted and the work of the enemy destroyed.

I realize that you may not be able to locate people or have a physical discussion or confrontation. However, I am suggesting that you examine your core and confront those unresolved issues within. In your confrontation process, you must first forgive and then let go. As long as you hold on to hurts and violations, you will remain in bondage.

Remember that Satan is the enemy and the author of all destruction. He is not going to surrender a stronghold. You must pull it down! *"For the weapons of our warfare are not carnal, but mighty through God to the pulling down of strong holds"* (2 Cor. 10:4).

FACING SHAME

"There is therefore now no condemnation to them which are in Christ Jesus, who walk not after the flesh, but after the Spirit" (Rom. 8:1). This is the scripture that you should show the enemy when he bomb-rushes you with shame. *Shame* deals with the way you view yourself. It is defined in Webster's Dictionary as a "painful emotion caused by consciousness of guilt." This means that you are experiencing additional hurt that comes because you are actually thinking about the bondage that you were connected to.

Please understand that whenever you dig up old stuff and

expose it to God or anyone else (including yourself), you may face a season of shame. This is the feeling you get when you walk into a building and begin to feel as though everyone is staring at you (because they know what you did). Shame will make you hold your head down, even when you have been forgiven. It will cut you down and keep you from going higher. I'm telling you, this season will run you all the way back!

The enemy's purpose of this season is to use your guilt and self-doubt as a weapon to get you to refuse your deliverance. He wants you to feel as though your sin was so bad that you are not worthy of God's mercy and grace. But you have to attack those thoughts by forgiving yourself and knowing that Jesus died for us while we were yet in our sins. Don't make yourself pay for anything that He has already paid for.

The thing about this season is that it can last a minute, a day, or forever. There is no time restraint because it's really up to you. The enemy has no right to bind you with shame. Therefore, once you really believe the Word of God and understand how to use it against him, this season will be over.

A few years ago, I was lying in bed thinking about an old relationship. I thought about how terrible it ended up for me and how offensive it was to God. This relationship almost took me out. Then, out of the blue, I started crying and thinking that I was so awful that nothing could help. The enemy began telling me that I was too bad off to be renewed by God. And after I listened to him and constantly pressed the rewind button in my head, I was totally depressed. It took hours for me to snap out of that.

Finally, I could hear the Spirit of the Lord say, *"The blood of Jesus has washed it all away."* So, I sat up and thought about the hymn *The Blood Will Never Lose Its Power.* I began to sing that song to myself. And when I made it to the part of the song that says, "It reaches to the highest mountain and flows to the lowest valley," I knew I was going to be okay. Eventually, I changed my thoughts from my past to the sacrifice that Jesus made for me. And, within minutes, it was all over. I made it through that little season of shame and gained the victory! Remember, this season ends when you end it. It's all in your control.

Brothers and sisters, this is how we have to fight through it. When the enemy keeps throwing your sins in your face, you have to counterattack very quickly, which means you must be prepared. First of all, memorize some scriptures. There will be times when your Bible will not be at your disposal. Secondly, learn some good old-fashioned hymns that contain words of comfort and encouragement. Finally, do not forget to pray. Remember, God is a very present help in time of trouble.

You have been forgiven. Forgive yourself now and move forward. And by all means, do not let anyone *look you into shame*! I know firsthand that people will stare at you so long and hard until you can actually feel their thoughts. But this is when you need to look straight at them with the confidence of knowing that you have been forgiven.

One day I saw a lady who looked familiar to me. I went to her and asked her if we knew one another. She said, "Oh yes, Lisa, we were church members for years." I asked, "Where are you attending church now?" And she replied, quite frankly I might add, "The house!" I said, "The house?"

She then explained that after attending our church, she was through with church folks and did not have time for "haters and crazy people." She went on to say that she certainly did not approve of the methods by which we accepted new preachers into the ministry. She said, "You all just let anybody preach, whether they are called or not." I said, "Well, you know I've been called." She replied, "See what I mean!"

Now, because I do have a sense of humor, my first reaction was to laugh. But when I thought about it, you know, I wanted to step back into the world of sin, give her a piece of my mind, and send her on her way! But I did not. I reminded myself that I had just told the lady I was a minister of the Gospel. Therefore, I gathered my thoughts and began to minister to her. Now, I could have just let her go on to the devil, or I could have fallen into a slump. But I took control of that situation, and I won.

The point is this: do not allow shame (brought upon you by

yourself or anyone else) to take you out. Fight through it. Trust me—you will never imagine how many times I wanted to take out different sections of this book. I did not feel good about sharing my weakness with the world. In fact, the devil is telling me right now to start deleting. But just as I have advised you, I have to tell him there is no condemnation for me, and I have no need to be ashamed of forgiven sins. And when I resist him, he flees.

Ultimately, I want you to remember that if you are facing this season of shame, you have the control key. When the thoughts come, you should begin to activate the following scripture: *"Whatsoever things are honest, whatsoever things are just, whatsoever things are pure, whatsoever things are lovely, whatsoever things are of good report; if there be any virtue, and if there be any praise, think on these things"* (Phil. 4:8). Take control of your thoughts and focus on good things. Think about all of the blessings of the Lord. Think about your daily benefits that are added. Think about something sweet and pleasant and just be ready to respond when the enemy returns.

DEVELOPING TRUST

If you are to ever walk in deliverance, you must learn to develop this season of trust. This season is twofold in that you must trust in God's ability to pull you out and sustain you as well as trust that you are capable of walking in deliverance. For some, this is a crucial step because people often base their ability to trust on earlier stages in their life when trust was either fully developed or severely damaged. This means that they either have a healthy heart and mind concerning trust, or their ability to trust was violated. The bottom line is that as you are moving through seasons of deliverance, you must develop a *trust* in God.

Webster's Dictionary defines *trust* as "assured reliance on the character, ability, strength, or truth of someone or something; dependence on something future or contingent." This means that if you are to develop trust in God, you cannot compare Him with any other person or broken experience that you may have encountered. You must allow Him to stand on His own character and strength. If you connect Him to the ability of any other person, your deliverance will be hindered.

Trust in God is absolutely necessary for deliverance because His role in your life is so broad. One minute, He may stand in as a friend. The next minute, He may allow you to experience a darkroom. At another time, He may chastise you. And without warning, He can shower you with unmerited favor. Therefore, you have to just trust His character. You must believe that in good times and in bad times He is still a loving God. You must understand that He will not harm you or allow you to suffer anything that you cannot bear.

I was saved for most of my life before I realized that I did not trust God with my total care. When my father died in 2002, I immediately felt uncovered and unprotected. To me, there were only two kinds of people in this world—those with fathers and those without. I had no clue that God could heal that type of hurt and even provide a covering for me.

Because I never trusted Him in this role, I had to work at developing this relationship with Him. I had to visualize God rushing in to save me or extending His hand of protection. I had to construct this relationship completely from scratch and become open to having God as my father. Now, since I have established that level of trust with Him, nothing can break that bond.

For those of you who may have a difficult time trusting God, you can start by reading and confessing scriptures on trust as well as revealing to Him vulnerable issues in your life. As you begin to apply the appropriate scripture to resolve those issues, you will see the Word of God come to life, and your level of trust in God will increase. Remember that as you are building this relationship with God, you must also trust yourself. You must believe that you can walk in the newness of His forgiveness and love. If you do not establish a love relationship with yourself, you will believe that you have to depend on someone else to complete you or help you get back up. You will begin to pray to God but will look to another for the answer. This same self-doubt will build paranoia that can send you back to what you are stepping out of.

Understand that you can stay delivered without other influences. You can make your own decisions and pray your own prayers. If you act like you need some other person in order to live, you will become dependent on them and not God. In fact, the Holy Spirit is urging me to say that your dependency on your pastor, mentor, best friend, or anyone else is a setup! If you don't watch it, you will set up an idol god and miss out on your destiny.

Believe it or not, God is going to show you some things that only you can see. Your network of friends may not see it, and you will need to trust what God said and step out on it.

You pick your own car. Buy the cookies you like to eat. Be friends with people that make you comfortable. If you like the shoes, buy them. Be yourself and stop being paranoid about your decisions. You are God's child, and He has equipped you with all you need to be successful. Make baby steps if necessary, but trust God and believe in who you are in Him. As you do so, try to incorporate into your life the action described in a quote I came across as I was working at my mother's desk one day:

> See for yourself. Listen for yourself. Think for yourself. Then you can come to an intelligent decision for yourself. It is good to keep wide-open ears and listen to what everybody else has to say. But when it is time to make the decision, you have to weigh what you have heard own its own

and place it where it belongs. Then, come to a decision for yourself. You will never regret it. (Anonymous)

DEALING WITH INTIMACY AND VULNERABILITY

The season of intimacy and vulnerability can be fun and sweet, but you have to be careful. Once you have built a level of trust in God and have worked through many of the major issues in your life, you may find yourself longing for intimacy, which can also lead to vulnerability. The tricky part is that if you do not find the intimacy that you desire, you may run into spiritual isolation or character concerns. This can be a deliverance block.

It is absolutely normal to long for intimacy. *Intimacy* is simply a desire to be in a relationship "marked by a warm friendship developing through long association" (Webster). It is when a person needs to feel connected to someone else. And when you have given up so much of your "old self," you will want something to fill in the blanks. This is when you have to really consider the Lord and wait on Him to set things up for you.

If you can just be patient, God is going to help you get on a new track with people or even with finding new hobbies and associations. Whatever you do, do not get frustrated and isolate yourself, even in spirituality.

As I went through deliverance, I had a deep desire to be intimate. However, instead of wanting intimacy with people, I wanted intimacy with God. The problem is that I wanted to be intimate with God and God alone. I desired to be in His presence all of the time. I could be in the mall or riding in my car, and I would push everything on speed to get home so that I could be with God. I wanted to be on my prayer blanket and just lift my hands and worship Him. I wanted to close my bedroom door and just sit in His presence. This was fine, but I also began to neglect everybody else. In other words, I became spiritually isolated.

Remember the lady who left my church because of her insecurities? Well, I ended up having to minister to her on the trap of isolation. You see, when she started having church at her house, she fell right into a trap. She became a Christian introvert. According to Webster's Dictionary, *introversion* is "the state or tendency toward being wholly or predominantly concerned with and interested in one's own mental life." When this happens, negative character issues may develop. You may become self-righteous, judgmental, or selfish, all of which can block your deliverance.

The devil knows that fellowship is crucial to Christian development, and when people cut themselves off from others, this aborts access to new information and revelations. It also aborts the opportunity for the people to develop positive patterns within themselves.

Do not misunderstand me. I know that some people like to be alone. This only becomes dangerous when they never come out.

If this is happening with you, it is time to investigate some things and begin to branch out a little. God wants you to see other people, learn from them, and even offer your gifts. Do not become wrapped up in a strange spiritual cocoon.

The other side to this is that the need for intimacy can also lead to vulnerability. When you become more spiritual, you may also become vulnerable. This means that you may begin to leave yourself open without a guard. In essence, you may lose the edge to protect yourself. But you must remember that even in the spiritual world, there are limits. Don't become so sweet and humble that you let people run you down.

If you realize that someone is not returning love, you should leave the relationship. I once heard a preacher say that if someone can leave you and not look back or can continuously cause you harm, then you need to have *the gift of goodbye*!

When I went through this season of vulnerability, I had the hardest time releasing people who meant me no good. I always wanted to hold on to what we had. If a friendship ended, I lost sleep trying to figure out how I could restore the relationship. I tried and tried. But now, I have *the gift of goodbye*. If you don't mean me any good, then by all means goodbye!

The point is the intimacy and vulnerability season is delicate. Make sure that you balance it all out. It is okay for you to desire intimacy with people and with God. But don't lose yourself in the process. Just be careful and stable-minded.

HEALING

Let's look at an anticipated season of this process of deliverance—healing. To heal means to be made whole or restored. Like the season of shame, the healing season is largely based on your personal involvement. Yes, God has the power to wipe all pain away. But He begins to manifest our healing as we begin to eliminate and initiate. We must eliminate all excuses of the past and present as well as initiate steps to building the future.

In Matthew, chapter 9, when the woman with the issue of blood encountered Jesus, her decision to eliminate all excuses of her current situation played a major role in her deliverance. This woman had to forgive those who did not help her through the rough times; she had to forgive the physicians who took her money and gave up on her; she had to release self-pity and self-doubt; and she had to fight through regrets, shame, rejection, and vulnerability. She had to resist the inclination to make justifiable excuses in order to press her way into the presence of Jesus where she knew she could be healed.

In Mark, chapter 10, when Bartimaeus desperately made his healing plea to receive of Jesus his sight, he also had to separate himself from all excuses. This man depended on the kindness of others and had to face the fact that he could not provide for himself. I have no doubt that his issues were so drastic that he could have told Jesus all about them. Yet, when the opportunity presented itself, Bartimaeus ignored the inconveniences of his life and immediately asked for and received his healing.

When I wanted to be healed of the hurt that damaged my spirit and the harm that came along with sin, I, too, had to leave all excuses behind, regardless of how legitimate I thought them to be. I had to turn them all in. When this was done, I was positioned for healing.

The same must be true for you. When you are ready to initiate and move through a season of healing, you must also be willing to get rid of all excuses. You cannot hold on to emotional and physical abuse, betrayal, neglect, or defeat. You have to let it go and get into a position for healing.

Let's look at Bartimaeus again. He could have waited for Jesus to come to him and demonstrate the compassion that was obviously needed. Nevertheless, he initiated his own healing. This is what got Jesus' attention. In other words, when Jesus saw his determination, He was willing to release His power of healing. The same is true for us. God knows when we are ready to be healed. He can look at our hearts and see whether we have forgiven, released, forsaken all excuses and are ready to receive the healing that He has in store for us.

As stated earlier, your personal involvement in this process plays a major role in your healing. I pray that you will be able to receive it and walk in it. It is the Father's good pleasure to heal you. In fact, your healing is already there. Take advantage of the Word and initiate your future!

> *Bless the Lord, O my soul: and all that is within me, bless his holy name. Bless the Lord, O my soul, and forget not all his benefits: Who forgiveth all thine iniquities; who healeth all thy diseases; Who redeemeth thy life from destruction; who crowneth thee with loving kindness and tender mercies; Who satisfieth thy mouth with good things; so that thy youth is renewed like the eagle's. (Ps. 103:1–5)*

BEING SET FREE

"Being then made free from sin, ye became the servants of righteousness" (Rom. 6:18). Only those who have been bound can truly explain what it is like to be set free. Being set free is like receiving that first breath of air after you have been fiercely choking on an object or have been forced to remain under water for a dangerously extended period of time. In either case, there is a smothering feeling that makes every part of you panic and respond as if you are fighting to live. Then, at the last second, you receive air. You breathe. In other words, you live! Being free means you were dead but are now alive.

I can easily tell you about how sweet it is to be free, but it is difficult to do so without referring to the depth of the bondage. The two must go together. When God wanted to extend His hand of mercy and deliverance toward Jerusalem, He first told the prophet Ezekiel, *"Son of man, cause Jerusalem to know her abominations"* (Ezek. 16:2, NKJV). In other words, God needed the people to really understand the depth of their bondage so that they could appreciate the cost of being set free. Ezekiel 16:3–6 offers an allegorical description of what we were like before being made free:

> *Thus says the Lord God to Jerusalem: Your birth and your nativity are from the land of Canaan; your father was an Amorite and your mother a Hittite.*
>
> *As for your nativity, on the day you were born your navel cord was not cut, nor were you washed in water to cleanse you; you were not rubbed with salt nor wrapped in swaddling cloths.*
>
> *No eye pitied you, to do any of these things for you, to have compassion on you; but you were thrown out into the open field, when you yourself were loathed on the day you were born.*
>
> *And when I passed by you and saw you struggling in your own blood, I said to you in your blood, 'Live!' Yes, I*

said to you in your blood, 'Live!' (NKJV)

Even developing a mental picture of this passage is gruesome. The thought of being helpless, defenseless, and choking in
your blood is dreadful. But this describes what we were like before
deliverance. When we were slaves to sin, it was just like lying in
the streets, exposed and experiencing a slow and ugly process of
death. We were helpless, hopeless, and choking on our sin. The
nastiness of adultery, idolatry, strife, and uncleanness covered our
bodies with shame. We were drenched in slime and grit and separated from anything or anybody that could offer a hand of mercy.

The enemy was our master, and we were slaves to his purpose. He told us what to think, and we thought it. He told us who
to hate, and we hated them. He taught us how to stand puffed up in
pride, and we did that, too. He taught us how to be hypocrites, and
we mastered that as well. Ultimately, because the *wages of sin is
death*, we were going to die and spend eternity in a burning hell.

*"For when ye were the servants of sin, ye were free from
righteousness"* (Rom. 6:20). This means that even when the choice
of evil and good was presented before us, we were so messed up
that we were violently driven to choose evil. Our character and
purpose for living could not even conceive righteousness or the
ways of Jesus Christ. This is the drive that brought about addictions, murder, fornication, and backstabbing.

The stain of sin and bondage is so strong and fiercely against righteousness that one who is bound has no authority or power of himself to fight against it. This is why the blood of Jesus has to purge our conscience, and the Word of God must be a two-edged sword that cuts to the very core.

We can catch a glimpse of real bondage in the life of the man who was tortured by demons (see Luke 8:28–29). This evil force drove the man into cutting himself, running around the city naked and completely insane. He was so messed up that he refused to live in a house. He preferred living in the graveyard. Another glimpse of bondage can be seen in the life of the woman who claimed to be a soothsayer (see Acts 16:16). As Paul and Silas ministered throughout the city, she followed them and began to shout and declare that they indeed were men of God. Indeed they were, but the enemy used her as a distraction to try to stop their mission.

Well, just as Jesus rebuked the devil that held that insane man captive, Paul, in the name of Jesus, rebuked the devil that held that soothsayer captive. Both were under a power that was so strong that they were literally slaves to the enemy and did not have control over their own lives.

Those stories may sound far away and detached from our world. However, the same enemy that held those two captive is the power of darkness that makes us profess to be anointed vessels but walk in whoredom.

It's the same enemy that allows us to sing and preach yet encourages us to walk in pride. No, you may not look insane or even try to cause physical harm to yourself. But if you are walking in sin, it's from the same power of darkness. And until you are set free, you are operating under that same evil influence.

"No eye pitied you, to do any of these things for you, to have compassion on you; but you were thrown out into the open field" (Ezek. 16:5, NKJV). This scripture really explains the hatred that the enemy has for you. He will use you, abuse you, and leave you to hang in the open for all men to see. He will do whatever it takes to expose any inner hang-ups. He will use them to destroy your reputation, make you lose your respect among men, and bring shame upon anyone associated with you. But God, in His tender mercies and ability to deliver, is waiting to set you free:

> *'When I passed by you again and looked upon you, indeed your time was the time of love; so I spread My wing over you and covered your nakedness. Yes, I swore an oath to you and entered into a covenant with you, and you became Mine,' says the Lord God.* (Ezek. 16:8, NKJV)

God makes a covenant with those who are willing to walk out of sin. He offers His love and vows to become the Protector and true Master of those who will surrender. This means that you will not have to worry about suffering any repercussions of walking away, nor will you have to worry about being snatched out of God's hands. Once you make the vow with Him, you are His, and He keeps you in His care.

If you are bound in a physically or emotionally abusive relationship, or even if you are the abuser, you can run out of that relationship right into the arms of Jesus. There will be no repercussions with Him. He will not deny you. God will accept you and set you free. God is waiting to forgive you and cover you with His strong arm of protection. Once you enter into His love, no weapon that is formed against you will ever prosper again.

"Then I washed you in water; yes, I thoroughly washed off your blood, and I anointed you with oil" (Ezek. 16:9, NKJV). Being set free is when God, the Almighty God, has washed and cleansed you with His hands of compassion. With the powerful blood of Jesus, God washes off the stain, guilt, and grip of the enemy and lifts you up as a new creation. He then anoints or empowers you to go forth in the real work of the Kingdom and of your destiny.

"I clothed you in embroidered cloth and gave you sandals of badger skin; I clothed you with fine linen and covered you with silk" (Ezek. 16:10, NKJV). Not only will God anoint you, but He will also restore your dignity. He will give to you the clothing and covering that is fit for kings and queens. Those who knew you in

the past will not even recognize you. You will lose your look of bondage and will begin to look like royalty.

Let me give you a real life example. Just recently, I took my first trip to the hospital to pray for a young lady who used to attend my church. I was a little uncomfortable because I never had the boldness to visit the sick and pray for them. However, the unusual thing about this visit was that her mother told me that people often compared the young lady to me. And as she began to share the details of the comparison, I realized that those people thought that we were both women who were not completely sold out to God, straddling the fence.

There I was, standing as a missionary and staring my past in the face at the same time. It was a strange feeling, and my first human emotion was to be sad. Then, before I could think anything else, the mother began to say that some of those people who made the comparison about our former lifestyles were the same ones who told her to call me so that I could pray for the daughter and mentor her. The mother even went on to tell me that when she looks at me, she sees a different Lisa, one who is clearly changed and anointed. When she told me these things, I knew that God had restored the years that the cankerworm ate. He literally changed my name, put fine linen on me, and restored my dignity.

On any other occasion, I probably would not have even listened so carefully to what someone was saying about me. But this time was different. This time I was listening to a real witness because she knew me before I was set free. She was able to say, "I know what I saw a year ago, and I know what I see today!" Saints, I am telling you, when you surrender, those who knew you before will say, "Was not this the one who was naked and crazy?" And the response will be, "Yes, but this person is now clothed and in his right mind!"

God promises to dress you with beautiful jewelry and change your whole look. He vows to make you adorable again and noticeable among all of those who knew you before He took control. Trust me. Nobody can fix you up the way God can. He is going to bring you up from the ashes and the dunghill and set you among the princes of the land. And don't let anyone fool you. He is going to set you free and make your name great!

Romans 6:6, 11 records that *"our old man is crucified with him, that the body of sin might be destroyed, that henceforth we should not serve sin...Likewise reckon ye also yourselves to be dead indeed unto sin, but alive unto God through Jesus Christ our Lord."* When Jesus Christ died on the cross and rose from the dead, that sacrifice made us free. That gave us the right to stand up, look at whatever kept us bound, and cut those chains off forever.

This is why Paul says, *"I speak after the manner of men because of the infirmity of your flesh: for as ye have yielded your members servants to uncleanness and to iniquity unto iniquity;*

even so now yield your members servants to righteousness unto holiness" (Rom. 6:19). When we are made free through Jesus Christ, we become obligated to walk in righteousness. We are joined together in covenant with God, and the members of our body must yield themselves only to holiness. Then and only then can you know what it is like to really be free!

Being delivered and set free is to be free of the enemy's control and to be submitted to the control of our Lord and Savior, Jesus Christ. It is to be conformed to His image and renewed with His mind. For me, it is knowing that I can live in a world that is so confused and ever-changing and still know that I will be okay. It is knowing that the work that I offer in the name of the Lord will last forever and add to God's Kingdom.

It is knowing that I am in constant fellowship with the only wise God. It is knowing that He hears my voice, and that I hear His voice. It is knowing that no matter how bound I was, I have an advocate who is forever praying for me. It is knowing that I can now live! My sisters and brothers, you can live, too!

Dear Father,

We thank You for the miracle of being delivered and set free. We repent and turn away from those things that once held us bound, and we offer ourselves as a living sacrifice to You. Although we may have some leftover scars from our past, we pray that the blood of Jesus will wash them all away and reveal to our own eyes a new and perfect creature in You.

Cause our ears to hear and recognize Your voice and our eyes to see Your way. Let our feet be swift to follow You and let our hands be swift to do Your work.

We are surrendered vessels, and we offer our bodies as a living sacrifice to You, holy and acceptable for the upbuilding of Your Kingdom.

Reveal and remove anybody who is sent from the enemy to draw us back and surround us with people that You choose.

As we become renewed through Your Word and through prayer, open our minds that we may fully understand how to interpret Your instructions and apply them to our daily walk with You.

Teach us how to sacrifice for You and show us how to please You. Let Your will be done in our lives and forever be glorified through us.

Open the doors for our complete success and set us free to soar through this land as Your new and beautiful men and women.

We ask these things and believe in faith that You have heard and answered our prayers.

In Jesus' name,
Amen.

PART VI

WHILE YOU WAIT

SOMETHING SPECIAL HAPPENS WHEN YOU HAVE GONE THROUGH A PROCESS OF DELIVERANCE. YOU BEGIN TO SEE THINGS IN A DIFFERENT LIGHT. THE PAIN LEVELS OUT, AND YOU ARE MORE COMFORTABLE WITH THE IDEA THAT GOD STILL WANTS TO USE YOU.

HOWEVER, STEPPING OUT OF BONDAGE INTO DELIVERANCE CAN BE A SHOCK.

YOU ARE FREE.

THERE ARE NO MORE CHAINS.

THERE ARE NO MORE EXCUSES, AND YOU MAY NOT KNOW WHAT TO DO NEXT.

THIS SECTION TELLS YOU WHAT TO DO WHEN THERE IS NOTHING TO DO. IT'S SIMPLE: GATHER YOUR THOUGHTS, GET YOURSELF TOGETHER, AND JUST W.A.I.T.

SEVENTEEN

WHILE YOU WAIT, W.A.I.T.

"But let patience have her perfect work, that ye may be perfect and entire, wanting nothing" (James 1:4).

After you have gone through a process of deliverance and have been anointed and appointed by God, you will need to find a quiet place in your spirit, take a minute, and just breathe. Don't try to run out and save the world or *lay hands* on everybody. You will need to go through a period of rest because God is going to use this time to develop within you the patience that yields the perfect work.

When God sent Samuel to anoint David as the next king of Israel, David did not immediately assume the position as king (see 1 Sam. 16). He could have easily become full of pride or anxious to assume the new position. However, David went back to the sheepfold and resumed his responsibilities. God knew that David was the man for the job, yet He also knew that David needed to mature, build up a few testimonies and learn how to walk in His wisdom.

This required a period of waiting and occupying. During this phase, he continued to perfect the skills that he already had; he encountered and won a few battles over man and beasts; and he also offered himself as a servant, all of which were a part of God's plan. This is why waiting is an absolute.

One Sunday morning, I made the decision to fully surrender to my call into the ministry. I took a few deep breaths and made the bold step to tell my pastor. This was major because I knew that after I confessed it to him, he then had the authority to launch me out. In other words, play time was over. Although the confession felt like it lasted two hours, it only took two minutes. And just when I started to take a huge sigh of relief, he immediately walked inside the sanctuary and announced it to the church! Needless to say, I could have fainted!

After the announcement was made, I started experiencing anxiety attacks because I thought that he was going to schedule me to deliver a message soon. But just like David the shepherd boy, I began to experience the waiting phase. I was not asked to do a trial message. I was not asked to sing at anybody's church. In fact, for several months, I was not asked to contribute my gifts in any kind of way, to do anything for anybody.

The normal reaction was to become a little restless about not moving forward in the ministry. However, instead of fighting to stand on a platform, I used the time to get to know the Lord a little better. I started a daily prayer schedule and began to fast regularly. I made a decision to wait until God released me.

This is what you have to do as well. There will be times when there is nothing for you to do. Nobody will call your name, and people may even forget how "wonderful" you are. You will have to watch others be esteemed greater than you. You may even watch them establish the same kind of ministry that God has assigned to you. But you must still sit patiently and wait. If you move too soon, you will fail at what you are called to do, and you will also open the door for jealousy. This is why you have to W.A.I.T. To help you through this period, here is an acronym that you can use as a guide:

Wisdom	—	Seek the wisdom of God
Attitude	—	Obtain a new attitude
Increase	—	Increase in the knowledge
Timing	—	Accept God's timing

WISDOM

"Get wisdom, get understanding: forget it not; neither decline from the words of my mouth. Forsake her not, and she shall

preserve thee: love her, and she shall keep thee" (Prov. 4:5–6). As defined in Webster's Dictionary, *to be wise* is to possess "inside information; exercise sound judgment; have the ability to discern inner qualities and relationships; to demonstrate good sense." If you are going to survive the assignment that is on your life, you must begin to diligently seek the wisdom of God. This is done when you pray and ask God to give you wisdom. It is also done when you begin to study His patterns of actions as written in the Bible. This is crucial because your actions reflect whether or not you are walking in the wisdom that only comes from God.

When King Solomon took the throne, he wrote about the counsel that was given to him from his father, King David. David told Solomon that wisdom was the principal thing, and he must operate in the full understanding of God's instructions. In other words, before you make another move, before you preach another sermon, and before you start a ministry, the first thing that you must do is try to find out what God thinks about the situation.

David knew that God had the answer to everything. He also knew that when he followed the instructions of God, he won. And when he followed his own human intelligence, he lost. It was as simple as that. This is why he encouraged Solomon to seek wisdom from God. And for this same reason, I encourage you to use this waiting phase to seek wisdom. Only God can show you the inside information. Only God can show you how to avoid the traps of your enemy.

It is going to be wisdom that moves you to your next level, and wisdom will keep you there. *"Exalt her, and she shall promote thee: she shall bring thee to honour, when thou dost embrace her. She shall give to thine head an ornament of grace: a crown of glory shall she deliver to thee"* (Prov. 4:8–9).

Proverbs reminds us that only fools despise wisdom and instruction. And those who walk in God's wisdom will be elevated in the fullness of His glory. My brothers and sisters, do not make any moves before seeking the wisdom of God. His wisdom will tell you your next move. So, until you hear from Him, be still. Keep waiting, *"for wisdom is a defence, and money is a defence: but the excellency of knowledge is, that wisdom giveth life to them that have it"* (Eccles. 7:12). *"If any of you lack wisdom, let him ask of God, that giveth to all men liberally, and upbraideth not; and it shall be given him"* (James 1:5).

ATTITUDE

For years, I misunderstood the adage, "Your attitude will determine your altitude." I thought this meant that I had to be nice, always smile, and never get frustrated about issues. But really, this had very little to do with my frustration and my smile. This was a test of mindset, my position, my stance, and my thoughts concerning any particular issue. This means that if I believed that I was going to win, more than likely, I could experience a favorable out-come. And if I believed I would not be promoted, more than likely, I would not be. This is how the attitude determines the altitude, or how high you go.

When you are in this waiting phase, it is not important that you maintain a fake little smile. It is important that you maintain a Word-based attitude. You must begin to look at the issues of your life or ministry and say what the Word says about it. Once you know what God said about it, that fact must become your attitude or position on it. No matter how great the storm or how bizarre the situation becomes, your attitude must not be moved.

Imagine yourself playing a game of basketball, and before the game starts, you are told that you are on the winning team. Once this is told to you, this is the attitude that you must believe and maintain. Based on the inside information that you are aware of, you must declare and act as if you have already won the game. This means that even if your team falls behind by 20 or 30 points, you have used up all of your timeouts, and a few of the teammates were injured; you still need to know that when it's over, you will win! This is attitude, baby. It's believing what is true and not being moved.

Even as I was writing this book, there were times when I had no more than $23.00 in the bank. I drove a Mercedes Benz E320 and had no money for gas. However, my attitude is now based on the Word that says, *"God shall supply all your need according to his riches in glory by Jesus Christ"* (Phil. 4:19). This is the Word-based attitude that I stand on. This position allows me to look at a depleted checking account and see what it will be in the future. With this Word, I can easily see a million dollars! The wonder of it all is that I can recall at one time when I had the same amount in the bank, I wanted to die. This means that my attitude has greatly changed, and I am now seeing things the way God sees them. Hallelujah!

My brothers and sisters, take advantage of this waiting phase to change your perception and your attitude. Start calling the sick well. Start calling the poor rich. Start calling lack abundance. Start believing and standing firmly on the Word of God. You have to be able to look at terrible circumstances and know that you have already won! *Call those things that be not as though they were* (see Rom. 4:17).

INCREASE

"That ye might walk worthy of the Lord unto all pleasing, being fruitful in every good work, and increasing in the knowledge of God" (Col. 1:10). The "I" stands for "Increase." Increase or add to your knowledge base. You must start learning more. Study the Word, learn how to apply scriptures, go back to school, ask questions, take notes and pay attention. This is crucial to your devel-

opment. No matter what area you are gifted in, you have room to grow and a need to know more about it. This waiting phase is the perfect time. If you are to ever be effective in your ministry or any other area, you need to gain all of the knowledge that is available. Ignorance is not acceptable anymore.

"Study to shew thyself approved unto God, a workman that needeth not to be ashamed, rightly dividing the word of truth" (2 Tim. 2:15). Paul wrote these and other like scriptures in order to encourage Timothy, Titus, and the others to get themselves prepared for the work. He knew that those who were left to preach and teach would have to stand against scholars. This meant that they had to increase their knowledge base and be able to effectively communicate the Gospel of Jesus Christ. They could not just stand up, scan over scriptures, and automatically get men converted. No, they had to be prepared.

When God told me to write this book, I had no idea how to put this all together. However, I knew that God was not going to walk me to the library, find a book, log on the Internet, and print information on publishing books. No. He gave me the assignment, dropped the vision in my heart, put people in place to help me, and He expected me to get busy. I had to do all of the legwork. I used the computer, the library, and every other source to become knowledgeable in this area. I could have sat there and said, *"God, I have never written a book before. I do not know what to do."* And if I had done that, my whole life would have been on pause.

Even as I worked on the music that complements this book, I recall telling one of my producers to include me in the entire process. I wanted to know about studio costs and time, mixing and producing, publishing rights and royalties. I wanted to know it all. I understood that when God opens a door for you, ignorance is the main element that can block the progress.

One of the most tragic things I have seen among the saints is our laziness (of which I have been guilty so many times). We want God to do everything for us. It is so sad because all of us are sitting on awesome treasures. God has made some of us entrepreneurs, but we choose to sit there and give in to excuses and fear. We want Him to fill out the business loan application, magically make the loan officer give us the loan, clean up our credit, go find a building, write a business plan, and then bless it all. Well, that is just crazy. God expects us to do those things for ourselves. He has already promised to be with us and to open the door.

If God has called you to pastor a megachurch, you should begin studying megachurches. You should begin interviewing pastors who are already in that position, asking questions about managing that type of ministry, and visiting megachurches on Sundays and through the week. Find out how they manage thousands of dollars from week to week. You must increase your knowledge base in that area. Remember, to whom much is given, much is required. It would be a horrible thing if you acquired the church and lost it because you did not know how to manage it.

Do not misunderstand me; I know that God has the ability to just drop revelations out of the sky. But if we are really serious about moving forward, our actions should line up with that desire. I am not saying that we all must go to school and get a four-year degree. I am simply saying that in order to be more effective and have the tools to broaden your perimeter, you need to increase your knowledge base in that area. There are many ways to that, and it is up to you to find out which path is good for you. The point is this: God has provided you a period of downtime. If you were wise, you would use it to grow. And when you come out of this, you can come out swinging!

TIMING

By now, if you have experienced the rough parts of deliverance, you are ready to see a new day. You have lost some of the old passions and have gained new ones. You are now facing the light at the end of the tunnel and can see your healing, your new career, your new reputation, your new life! Now you must become a friend to the *timing* of God. You must realize that God's timing is perfect, and no matter how much you think you know about your life, you still do not know when the time is right:

To every thing there is a season, and a time to every purpose under the heaven:

A time to be born, and a time to die; a time to plant, and a time to pluck up that which is planted;

A time to kill, and a time to heal; a time to break down, and a time to build up;

A time to weep, and a time to laugh; a time to mourn, and a time to dance;

A time to cast away stones, and a time to gather stones together; a time to embrace, and a time to refrain from embracing;

A time to get, and a time to lose; a time to keep, and a time to cast away;

A time to rend, and a time to sew; a time to keep silence, and a time to speak;

A time to love, and a time to hate; a time of war, and a time of peace. (Eccles. 3:1–8)

Believe me, God knows when it is time to release you. He knows when the timing is perfect for you. You must continue to wait and begin to notice the changes that are now surrounding you. Pay attention to your mentors, watch the flow of the Spirit in your church, listen carefully to the sermons of your pastor, and take note of the scriptures that the Lord is bringing to your remembrance.

When these things begin to take a little twist, something is probably getting ready to happen.

My waiting phase was so long that I almost forgot what God said. And just when I thought I was out of time, on August 2, 2006, my pastor walked into the room where I was meeting with a few choir members and told me that I would have to deliver my first message in two weeks! My heart hit the floor, and I almost became ill. I'm telling you, this was like taking on Goliath.

Over the next two weeks, I tried to turn back on everything. I wanted to stop it all, and I even tried to negotiate with God one last time. The strange thing was that as people heard about it, they were walking up to me saying things like, "I'm waiting on a Word from God" and "I'm expecting a breakthrough." My thoughts were, "Who is going to give you all of that?" But I knew that this was the timing of God, and it would be perfect.

On August 16, 2006, I stood before a large group of people and released the message that God gave me. Because I had fasted, prayed, and studied, I was confident that the Lord had given me a message for the people. All I had to do was open my mouth and let the Lord use me. The Lord had promised that if I just walked to the microphone, He would anoint me and speak through me. This is what I depended on, and that is what He did.

I gained from that experience several powerful lessons that I will always take with me that I also believe will be helpful to you as you move into your next level of living. You will need to know some of the rewards that come with trusting God's timing:

- First, *it is very rewarding to know that you have followed through with God's command.* Obedience is the key when it comes to building the Kingdom and fulfilling your purpose.
- Second, *there is no reward like knowing that God used you to change minds, hearts, and lives.* This is the purpose of your anointing.
- Third, *when you obey God, you can see the promises of God brought to life.* It is when you make the move that you will be able to see the hand of God. He has no need to move when there is no working faith.

The point is this: God's timing is perfect. When you surrender and begin to walk in His will, there are benefits, and God will keep His end of the vow that He has made with you.

So, remember to just W.A.I.T., which means seek God's wisdom, get a new attitude, increase your knowledge, and trust God's timing. Believe me, your turn is coming! *"For yet a little while, and he that shall come will come, and will not tarry"* (Heb. 10:37).

Dear Father,

We thank You for teaching us to wait. We understand that pa-tience is a part of our walk with You, and that all things must be re-leased at Your perfect timing. We pray for opportunities to learn more of You as well as practice what we have learned. We pray that every moment be maximized and that no time will be spent in vain.

Please keep Your vision and plans for our lives before us and help us to tarry until it comes to pass. We will wait for You and continue to give You the glory.

In Jesus' name,
Amen.

PART VII

GREATNESS

BROTHERS AND SISTERS, WE HAVE FINALLY REACHED THE SECTION WHERE GOD RESTORES US, NOT AS WE WERE, BUT AS A NEW CREATION. THIS PART IS CENTERED ON THE LIFE OF THE HARLOT, RAHAB. WE WILL SEE HOW GOD CAN RECONSTRUCT WHAT WAS CONDEMNED.

REMEMBER, GOD NOT ONLY SAVES US, BUT HE RESTORES, REVIVES, AND RENEWS US. THIS POWER WAS EFFECTIVE FROM THE FOUNDATION OF THE WORLD, AND IT STILL WORKS TODAY.

AT THIS POINT, YOU CAN GRAB A CUP OF TEA, SIT BACK, RELAX, AND GET READY TO WITNESS A REAL DEMONSTRATION OF GOD'S LOVE AND REDEMPTIVE POWER. WATCH HIM SEND YOU BACK WITH A NEW NAME!

EIGHTEEN

THERE IS GREATNESS IN YOU

*"Ye are of God, little children, and have overcome
them: because greater is he that is in you,
than he that is in the world" (1 John 4:4).*

"There is greatness in you" is one of the latest themes that is used in the gospel world today. It goes right along with other themes like "It's your season" and "Get your inheritance." However, this one is a little different because, although many of us think that the *greatness* is our hidden gifts, talents, or callings, the true greatness is our *faith,* our unshaken belief in who God is as well as our ability to activate who God has made us.

God has given all of us grace and faith, and He has planted within us an awesome destiny. When we learn how to apply our faith to claim the things of God and to operate in His perfect will, we will then find ourselves launched into our season of purpose or into what I call a faith *journey of greatness*. This journey includes the sting of greatness, the call to greatness, and, ultimately, the walk of greatness.

"By faith the harlot Ra'-hab perished not" (Heb. 11:31). Who better can lead us into this journey than the harlot, Rahab? Now, I know that there were many others who walked in greatness, but I believe that in order for us to stay focused on this path of deliverance, we must take a look at one who walked in a certain degree of desperation yet possessed unwavering faith.

A GLANCE AT RAHAB

When Joshua became the new leader of the Israelites and was ready to move forward and possess the land of Jericho, he sent two spies into the city. When the spies arrived at Jericho, they found a place of lodging in a harlot's house. This house belonged to Rahab (see Josh. 2).

When you think of a harlot, or prostitute, you may visualize one who dresses in fishnet stockings, spike heels, and gaudy jewelry. You might also picture her wearing tight leather miniskirts and revealing blouses. Many people may picture a ruthless woman with no conscience who simply serves as a fantasy and ultimately destroys happy homes. Some may even imagine her to be uneducated, weak-minded, and clueless to her purpose and destiny.

There could be a number of unattractive descriptions for a harlot. But for some reason, I just do not believe that Rahab would fall under those descriptions. I do not think she walked the streets of the downtown area or waited at truck stops to solicit from desperate men.

On the contrary, I believe that Rahab was a harlot but not stereotypical. I think she was an intelligent woman who was very influential in her family and had clout in the community. She kept a clean house and fragranced it with the best oils that money could buy. I believe she was skilled and had the ability to perform at any level.

Yes, my friend. Rahab was a regular person. Had she lived during this time, she could have been the neighborhood aunt who cooked fresh vegetables and tender roast beef. Her refrigerator would be covered with pictures of children, family, friends, and cute little notes. Her pantry would be filled with goodies. Chocolates, cookies, and chips would be placed throughout in seasonally decorated bowls.

She could have been the executive who wore silk wraps, tailored suits and brand name shoes, and carried exclusive handbags. Her hair would have been freshly treated, and her nails would have been perfectly manicured. For the most part, she would have been able to function sociably around anybody. She would have been so composed that even though others knew about her sinful secret lifestyle, they would still envy her.

But for Rahab, in spite of a life of prostitution, a sting of greatness stirred within her soul. Thank God for the sting.

NINETEEN

THE STING OF GREATNESS

"Then I said, I will not make mention of him, nor speak any more in his name. But his word was in mine heart as a burning fire shut up in my bones, and I was weary with forbearing, and I could not stay" (Jer. 20:9).

A sting is defined as "a sharp or stinging element, force, or quality" (Webster). It causes discomfort and uneasiness. Particularly, the sting of greatness is felt when your inner faith in God and your understanding of who you really are in Him begin to disturb you as you are participating in something outside of God's will.

It becomes a pain that reminds you that you are going in the opposite direction of your potential. This means that the very thing that is meant to deliver you has become the element that causes you pain. It's the sting of greatness.

On the surface, Rahab appeared to be content. But a sting of greatness never allowed her to be completely happy. It caused her to stay up many nights imagining herself living a better life. She longed for her own special relationship and husband. She felt the need to have real intimacy and even have her own children. And even though this night life was profitable, she really wanted to be detached from it.

As she prepared for each night, the sting would begin to stir up and aggravate her soul. As she set the atmosphere for clients, she could feel the sting piercing at the very core of her spirit. As she oiled her body and slipped into a negligee, the sting would begin releasing whispers and even visions of her destiny.

Have you ever been in those shoes? Have you ever committed to something that was out of God's will, yet you could still feel the sting of greatness? I can recall one particular time when I had a casual friendship with someone I met during a weak time in my life. We were never intimate, but he always offered to cheer me up or to just be a "friend." Although I knew deep down that I was not interested in him, I continued to answer his calls. One day, as we were talking, he said that he loved the way that I walked and wished that I would make a special effort to walk for him. Of course, I was thinking, *"Oh Lord, this man is crazy,"* and I did not think much more about it.

Then, one day, I actually met him to have a social chat, and he made this strange walking request again. This time, I got out of my car and began to walk around the parking lot showing off and acting silly. But suddenly, as I was returning to the car, I heard the Holy Spirit ask me, *"What are you doing?"* I instantly stopped and began to look around because I felt ashamed. Then, as if that was not bad enough, I began to feel the sting of greatness stirring within me. It was rushing me back to my car and telling me that I must never compromise my integrity.

As I immediately left and was on my way home, the Lord continued to teach me about having a firm faith that could not be moved in any circumstance. He reminded me that I must be steadfast, unmovable, and always abounding in His work, never forgetting that I was anointed to do a mighty work in the Kingdom.

Brothers and sisters, do not be dismayed when you, too, experience a sting of greatness. It is going to be painful and maybe even embarrassing, but this is when you should thank God because this means that no matter what you do, you will not be able to get away from God's perfect will. This means that you have been marked and that you must step into the duty that God has assigned to you. It also means that soon and very soon the sting of greatness will give way to the *call to greatness*. Just do what Rahab did. Answer the door!

TWENTY

THE CALL TO GREATNESS

"And the Lord came, and stood, and called as
at other times, Samuel, Samuel. Then Samuel answered,
Speak; for thy servant heareth" (1 Sam. 3:10).

When you have been called to greatness, the Lord is actually challenging you to use your faith to function in a higher position or authority. At this point, the Holy Spirit begins a strong campaign to change your way of thinking, pull you out of a poverty mentality, and point you into the direction of your destiny.

Oftentimes, what happens during this call to greatness is that you may experience a series of extraordinary things. You may have to go to places where you have never been. You may have to talk with people you never thought you would need. You may have to receive assistance and leadership from sources you never thought you would submit to.

You may even have to open your front door and entertain your own enemy in order to get to that place. Rahab was in this phase of the journey when she let the spies into her home. I believe that she knew her time was near, and that her inner faith was just about to pay off:

> *And it was told the king of Jericho, saying, Behold, there came men in hither to night of the children of Israel to search out the country.*
>
> *And the king of Jericho sent unto Ra'-hab, saying, Bring forth the men that are come to thee, which are entered into thine house: for they be come to search out all the country.* (Josh. 2:2–3)

When the two spies knocked on Rahab's door, she defied her own king and country to make her next move into her destiny. This leads us into our first point: *don't let anyone stop you from answering the call. Despite the king, take the risk!*

At this juncture, Rahab's king was standing between her life and her death. I can imagine that in a split second, she looked at her current lifestyle and instantly decided to defy her king, her country, and risk her life to be free. So, she told the officers, *"The men came to me, but I did not know where they were from"* (Josh.

2:4, NKJV).

Many times, we skip over the fact that Rahab's decision to lie to the armed forces in her country was detrimental. This one decision could have killed her and her entire family. This lets us know that she understood her time, and it did not matter who she had to defy in order to move into her destiny.

Brothers and sisters, there is going to come a time when you, too, may have to stare the king in your life in the face and defy him! I don't care who or what the king is. It could be a habit. It could be a thirty-year-old useless relationship. It could be a job. It could be a church. Whatever it is, if it is in the way, you must defy it. I understand that this will not be easy. This could very well mean that you may lose your house, car, or even a relationship. But don't let anything stop this process. You are almost there!

Please understand that whatever it is and whoever it is, God has already prepared a way of escape for you. Look at that king and take the risk! This could be a life and death decision.

Further, when the two spies knocked on Rahab's door, technically, they were her enemies. Remember, they were spies sent from the army of Israel who had all intentions of destroying everyone in Jericho, including her. But isn't this just like God to use your enemies to propel you into your expected end? You see, when you have greatness in you, even your enemies will be drawn to assist and bless you.

"But she had brought them up to the roof of the house, and hid them with the stalks of flax, which she had laid in order upon the roof" (Josh. 2:6). Rahab had to think quickly. She had to make a decision to risk her life. Then she had to make a decision to treat her enemies with special care. This reveals the next important point: *never be afraid of your enemies, but treat them as friends.*

When there is a call on your life, you must not use any time fighting your enemies. I do not care if they drag your name through the mud and hang it on the highway. You must not be moved. You have to understand that God is able to make even your foes bless you. The only way they will win is if you try to fight them back. Therefore, you must do what Rahab did—agree quickly with your adversaries.

As you are on this journey of greatness, you will have many enemies. In fact, people who you thought were your friends may even become your enemies. It seems that people are more comfortable with you when you are dying in the hands of Satan. You see, people understand that you will never surpass them in terms of prosperity and spiritual growth as long as you are playing church. But when you get serious with God, there is no limit!

Jesus has instructed us to love our enemies and bless them. More than likely, your enemies will be among those who will push you to your next place in God. They will force you to read the Bible, seek God's face, and pray. I'm telling you—use your enemies to bless you:

> *And before they were laid down, she came up unto them upon the roof;*
>
> *And she said unto the men [the spies], I know that the Lord hath given you the land, and that your terror is fallen upon us, and that all the inhabitants of the land faint because of you.*
>
> *For we have heard how the Lord dried up the water of the Red sea for you, when ye came out of Egypt; and what ye did unto the two kings of the Am'-or-ites, that were on the other side Jordan, Si'-hon and Og, whom ye utterly destroyed.*
>
> *And as soon as we had heard these things, our hearts did melt, neither did there remain any more courage in any man, because of you: for the Lord your God, he is God in heaven above, and in earth beneath.* (Josh. 2:8–11)

Jesus has instructed us to speak to the mountain and command it to move. This means that once you find out what God says about the situation, you must then activate your faith and speak the change into existence. Based on what you have heard about God, tell your trouble it has to go!

In this case, everything that Rahab did was based on what

she knew about God. This is why she had strength and did not understand it. She had faith and did not understand it. All she knew was that she believed in God, even before the two spies entered her house. That is why she was able to speak it so quickly when they showed up. She was eager to tell them that she knew they were going to win, and that she wanted to be on their team. Rahab's time had arrived. She was finally going to get her change!

Next, Rahab began to use this situation to her advantage:

> *Now therefore, I pray you, swear unto me by the Lord, since I have shewed you kindness, that ye will also shew kindness unto my father's house, and give me a true token:*
> *And that ye will save alive my father, and my mother, and my brethren, and my sisters, and all that they have, and deliver our lives from death. (Josh. 2:12–13)*

This brings us to the final point: *when you come out, bring somebody with you!*

It is not enough for us to get our deliverance and just begin to live a happy life. We must remember that God is not selfish, and His plan is for all of His children to be saved and working in His Kingdom. In fact, this is why He saves us. He saves us so that we can then work to save others.

If you have been delivered, you should find a way to help

deliver others who are still entangled. Because you have gone through this process, you already know how to be set free. James 4:17 says, *"Knowing what is right to do and then not doing it is sin"* (TLB). God needs you to pull them out!

You must become an intercessor, one who acts or intervenes on behalf of another person. This is a sure sign that you have matured in Christ and that you have the love of God abiding within you. *"But whoso hath this world's good, and seeth his brother have need, and shutteth up his bowels of compassion from him, how dwelleth the love of God in him?"* (1 John 3:17). Above all, the love of God must be shown through your intercession and giving. This is one of the main keys to keeping yourself delivered!

Intercession is a powerful tool. Rahab locked in her requests for those who were at risk. This is the attitude we must have once we have been delivered. Go get your family! Go get your friends! And if you really want to be radical for Christ, go get your enemies! You have the power to pray them through!

When you pray for others, someone will pray for you. When you give others money, someone will give to you. When you encourage others, someone will exalt you up.

I am stressing this point because you need this element of intercession working as you are trying to remain free. This will keep you from being selfish, and it will also ensure that God will use others to do the same for you. Jesus said, *"Give, and it shall be given unto you; good measure, pressed down, and shaken together, and running over, shall men give into your bosom. For with the same measure that ye mete withal it shall be measured to you again"* (Luke 6:38).

TWENTY-ONE

THE WALK OF GREATNESS

*"And I will put my spirit within you, and cause
you to walk in my statutes, and ye shall keep my judgments,
and do them" (Ezek. 36:27).*

When you step out of a life of destruction and declare to walk with the Lord, God will turn your life around completely! Not only will He save you, but He will restore you to a greater place of authority in Him and even use you to give birth to greatness:

Joshua said unto the people, Shout; for the Lord hath given you the city.

And the city shall be accursed, even it, and all that are therein, to the Lord: only Ra'-hab the harlot shall live, she and all that are with her in the house, because she hid the messengers that we sent. (Josh. 6:16–17)

But Joshua had said unto the two men that had spied out the country, Go into the harlot's house, and bring out thence the woman, and all that she hath, as ye sware unto her.

And the young men that were spies went in, and brought out Ra'-hab, and her father, and her mother, and her brethren, and all that she had; and they brought out all her kindred, and left them without the camp of Israel. (Josh. 6:22–23)

When Joshua took the city of Jericho, it was Rahab's faith, commitment, and intercession that made him remember her. This same greatness delivered her and her family!

As we know, Rahab continued to live among the Israelites and, eventually, married and gave birth to Boaz, the famous rich man who married Ruth. Rahab is listed in Jesus' lineage and in the hall of fame of great faith! Like Rahab, who started out as a harlot, an anointed whore, by faith in God all of God's children can receive the great things He has in store!

May God bless you and take you to a place that can only be revealed, defined, and sustained by Him.

Dear Father,

As we have reached the end of this journey, I pray that somebody's heart has been changed or returned to You. I ask that this instrument has powerfully exposed the enemy so that we can be prepared to counteract with Your biblical principles and instructions for a successful life.

Help us not to be judgmental towards anyone so that the Holy Spirit can assist us in searching within our own hearts, motives, and actions.

Lord, I pray that we will become empowered through Your Word and through the blood of Jesus so that we can be healed, delivered, and set free to serve You. Help us to be bold Christians as well as bold intercessors for those who are still at risk. Surround us with those who can pray for us and continue to cover us with Your mercy and grace.

"Now unto him that is able to keep you from falling, and to present you faultless before the presence of his glory with exceeding joy, To the only wise God our Saviour, be glory and majesty, dominion and power, both now and ever" (Jude 24–25).

In Jesus' name,
Amen.

NOT AS A SERVANT BUT A BROTHER BELOVED

Sometimes, we have the most difficult time trying to live and thrive around those who knew us before we were delivered. It seems that all they recall is what we were and what we used to do. Some will try to convince us that we have not changed, and others will even attempt to send us right back to our old status. But Jesus said, *"If the Son therefore shall make you free, ye shall be free indeed"* (John 8:36). This statement is without repentance and does not need the approval of men. It is an absolute promise that always stands as is. If you have been set free by Jesus, then you are still free!

Another precious point about your new life is that when you return to your home and to those who surround you, you will not return as you were. You will be on a new level in God, and you will begin to function in a new authority. The story of Onesimus, as recorded in Philemon, is a great example of how deliverance and restoration make room for a new level in God.

This book is a personal letter written by Paul to Philemon, a wealthy master who lived in Colossae. Paul wrote this letter on the behalf of Onesimus, a former slave of Philemon's. When Onesimus was a slave, he betrayed his master by stealing from him and escaping to Rome. As he was on the run, he met Paul, became a converted Christian, and, eventually, a devoted witness for Jesus Christ.

As time passed, Paul wanted Onesimus to stay longer with him in Rome, so he prepared him to return home and face the situation that he escaped from. The special part of this reunion is that Onesimus was no longer a thief. He had been changed, and he also had a letter of advocacy in his hand. Let's read a portion of it:

I appeal to you for my son Onesimus, whom I have begotten while in my chains,

who once was unprofitable to you, but now is profitable to you and to me.

I am sending him back. You therefore receive him, that is, my own heart,

whom I wished to keep with me, that on your behalf he might minister to me in my chains for the gospel.

But without your consent I wanted to do nothing, that your good deed might not be by compulsion, as it were, but voluntary.

For perhaps he departed for a while for this purpose, that you might receive him forever,

no longer as a slave but more than a slave—a beloved brother. (Philem. 10–16, NKJV)

This story is so powerful. It is a clear picture of how God mercifully saves us, delivers us, and restores us. Onesimus was wrong for stealing from his master and running away. But God had a plan. I am sure that Onesimus had no idea that he would run right into the arms of an apostle. This is why I know that God watches over us even as we are in a lost and sinful state.

The wonder of this story is the fact that Paul had two exceptional requests concerning the manner in which Onesimus should be received. First, he asked that Philemon would accept him as a beloved brother, not as the slave that he was. This meant that Onesimus should not wear any chains or perform any slave-like duties. He was to be considered an equal and released of any connections to his past.

Oh, my God! Do you see that? When God cleans you up and sends you back, you are not going back as a slave. You are going as a brother, elevated and now working in God's Kingdom. I don't care what you were before. You could have been a drug dealer, a compulsive gambler, a home wrecker, an abuser, a leach, an intimidator, a liar, or a thief. It does not matter. The fact is that when you return, your name will be changed, and you must be accepted as a brother. And by all means, do not accept any parts of your bondage. Walk in your new name and position!

Paul's next request was: *"If then you count me as a partner, receive him as you would me. But if he has wronged you or owes anything, put that on my account. I, Paul, am writing with my own hand. I will repay"* (Philem. 17–19, NKJV). By now, I know you are smiling and thanking God. This means that God will put some-one in place to help you repair your mistakes. Notice one thing: just because Onesimus was delivered did not mean that he had the right to overlook his debt. Instead, Paul offered to pay for Onesi-mus' debt.

This is how God works. He does not ask us to ignore any situation that we may have destroyed. He wants us to make peace with the situation, and then He will intervene with a miracle! Look at how he had Paul to stand in for this runaway slave who was also a thief. Not only was his name changed, but his debt was wiped away! This is what happens when you fully surrender and give your life to Jesus Christ. He sends you back greater than you were before!

All you have to do is stand on His Word and watch Him move on your behalf. Trust me, God will always come through for you. Now, after all of that has been said, let me be the first to say, *"Welcome home, brother."*

Dear Father,

Thank You for saving us, delivering us, and sending us back with a new name!

Thank You for who You are, who You are through us, and for all You have done for us.

In Jesus' name,
Amen.

I did not want to end this book without offering Jesus Christ to you. Without Him, we would have no purpose. The Plan of Salvation is submitted by Aurelia Jones-Smith.

THE PLAN OF SALVATION

"This is the stone which was set at nought of you builders, which is become the head of the corner. Neither is there salvation in any other: for there is none other name under heaven given among men, whereby we must be saved" (Acts 4:11–12).

The word "salvation" means "deliverance" or "rescue." You can be delivered or rescued from worldly dangers, but only by the blood of the Lamb, Jesus Christ, are we rescued from sin and its penalty, which is eternal death in hell fire, and reconciled into a right relationship with God to receive abundant and eternal life.

The Bible says in Ephesians 2:8 that *"by grace are [we] saved through faith; and that not of [ourselves]: it is the gift of God."* But even though salvation is a gift and not obtainable by our own works, we must nevertheless obtain it by our action.

"God so loved the world, that he gave his only begotten Son, that whosoever believeth in him should not perish, but have everlasting life" (John 3:16). The gift is free, but only *whosoever believeth in Him* (Jesus Christ) can be a recipient.

If we could believe in *anybody* or *anything* and still be

saved, we would have no need for a savior; and the blood of Jesus would have been shed in vain. But we needed a savior, and the Savior Jesus willingly gave His life for us.

In Acts 16:30, a man asks, "What must I do to be saved?" Romans 10:9 simply says:

- You must first *"confess with thy mouth the Lord Jesus."* It means to declare openly by way of speaking out freely as a result of deep conviction of facts. It is to say that you are convinced and no other doctrine can sway you, that no other argument can win you over, and nobody can change your mind that Jesus was sent from God the Father to save us and that He is God the Son.

- You must *"believe in thine heart that God hath raised him from the dead."* You must accept His death and resurrection as a fact and place your trust in Him, the risen Christ, who rose from the dead with all power in His hand. It means to place your confidence in Him, to rely upon Him, to commit to Him and to put your life into His hands. In other words, have faith in Him.

- And if these things are done, *"thou shalt be saved."*

If you want to receive Jesus Christ as your Lord and Savior, I invite you to repeat these words: "I believe in Jesus Christ and believe in my heart that He is raised from the dead." According to the Word of God, you are now *saved*.

My Prayer for You

Father,

In the name of our Lord and Savior Jesus Christ, we thank You for these who have now submitted themselves to You. Forgive their sins and have mercy upon their souls.

Thank You for the promise of the Holy Spirit, the Comforter and Guide, which each has received through faith in Christ Jesus. Conform them to the image of Your Son and transform them by the renewing of their minds. Lead them to a place of worship where the Gospel of Jesus Christ is preached and taught that their lives may be strengthened in Him. Help them to walk daily in the Spirit and not in the flesh that they might come to know Jesus in the power of His resurrection and the fellowship of His sufferings. Keep them in everlasting communion.

Finally, O Lord, keep them from falling to the temptations of Satan whose plan is only to steal, kill, and destroy.

Thank You, Lord, for hearing and answering our prayers. We love You, we bless You, we glorify and magnify You, and praise Your holy name.

We offer this prayer in Jesus' name,

Amen.

ACKNOWLEDGEMENTS

The task of writing this book required total commitment, seclusion, and spiritual transformation. Thus, I displayed some peculiar behavior. This is why I am grateful that the following individuals stood by my side.

First and foremost, I offer unconditional praise and thanksgiving to my God. I am still in awe of Your patience, provision, direction, and never-ending love that covered me day and night. Thank you, Jesus, the Living Word, for the sacrifice that made redemption and progress possible. And thank you, Holy Spirit. I realize that the only form of true praise to You is to live a life that demonstrates this deliverance message. To God be all of the glory.

I owe a special debt of gratitude to my mother, Maebell Williams Gibbs. Thank you for allowing me to be myself. I could only imagine what it must have been like as you contested the urges to guide my steps throughout this process. Yet, with compassion, love, and prayer, you simply watched it all unfold.

I have benefited from watching you demonstrate vigilance and strength as a mother, determination as a provider, and integrity as a woman. For that, I am eternally grateful. Thank you.

Special thanks are due to my sisters and brothers—Joann, Sherry, Mary, Ben, and Lee—who willingly gave me permission to

213

share some of our intimate stories. Thank you for making my life rich with substance, balance, fun, and laughter. I pray that each of you will walk in your full potential. You have so much to offer.

To my ever-supportive family of God, Pastor John C. Evans, Jr. and members of Cathedral African Methodist Episcopal Zion Church: thank you for your exceptional ability to nourish my spirit and extend heartening support.

To all of my friends and mentors: thank you for understanding me and pushing me to the limit! Honestly, this would have been much more difficult without you. May God bless you all.

I give thanks to my impressive editor, Galina Lobodina, who never complained once during this process: for your patience, excellent review, and for making me sound good. Because of you, I never had to worry about the logistics of this book. Thank you.

And to my editor and sister in Christ, Aurelia Jones-Smith: only God can justly reward you for your sacrifice and spiritual offering to this book. And only God can share with you the depth of my appreciation. Truly, I am not capable of doing so. With your expertise, incredible commitment, and total submission to the Holy Spirit, any missing pieces to the book were found!

Thank you for opening the doors to your home, listening for my heart in each page, praying with me and for me, and for loving me enough to say, "Lisa, that information goes in another book!" I am convinced that God has an immeasurable plan for you. And it is my prayer that He will release an immeasurable blessing! From my heart, thank you.

To the gifted Cornelius "C.C." Moore and the paramount musician Barry Bolden: there is no doubt in my mind that this project would not have been complete without you. Both of you immediately became a part of my vision and worked endlessly to bring it to life. I pray that God will take you beyond what you have prayed for! Thank you.

The final acknowledgement goes to those who purchased, read, and were changed by the message in this book. I wish you God's best!

Lisa D. Williams is an anointed minister of the Word and a powerful psalmist for the Lord Jesus Christ. As an exhorter, she is passionate about the salvation and deliverance of God's people, committing her hands to evangelizing, empowering, and equipping them for His purpose. She offers her musical gifts as the choir director and worship leader at Cathedral African Methodist Episcopal Zion Church (CAMEZ) in Jackson, MS.

Before pursuing a ministerial writing and recording career, a love for children inspired Dr. Williams to serve as an elementary teacher for six years and a principal for three. She earned a Bachelor of Arts degree in English, a Master of Science degree in Education Administration, and a Doctor of Education degree in Early Childhood Education at Jackson State University, Jackson, MS.

Dr. Williams is a recipient of the Mississippi Announcers Guild "Woman of Excellence" Award, the Jackson Mississippi Music Award for "Best Female Lead Singer," and the "Best Choir Director" Award from the same. She has served as lead vocalist on various CAMEZ projects and has performed background vocals for leading recording artists.

Dr. Williams' book *Anointed Whore* and music CD entitled *Complete in Him* offer a unique perspective concerning her struggles, heart's conviction, and deliverance to walk in the liberty that

God has promised all who believe in His Son, Jesus Christ. The book and CD deliver a resounding message of hope for all who truly desire to be set free.

To contact Dr. Lisa D. Williams:

Live Publishing, LLC.

P.O. Box 1622

Jackson, MS 39215

E-mail: lisadwilliams@live.com

Web site: www.lisawilliamsministries.com